Christopher Dunkin

Speech delivered in the Legislative Assembly by Christopher Dunkin

During the Debate on the Subject of the Confederation of the British

North American Provinces

Christopher Dunkin

Speech delivered in the Legislative Assembly by Christopher Dunkin
During the Debate on the Subject of the Confederation of the British North American Provinces

ISBN/EAN: 9783337183707

Printed in Europe, USA, Canada, Australia, Japan

Cover: Foto ©ninafisch / pixelio.de

More available books at **www.hansebooks.com**

PARLIAMENTARY DEBA..ES,

3RD SESSION, 8TH PARLIAMENT, CANADA.

———•———

SPEECH

DELIVERED IN THE LEGISLATIVE ASSEMBLY,

BY

CHRISTOPHER DUNKIN, ESQ.,

MEMBER FOR BROME.

DURING THE DEBATE ON THE SUBJECT OF THE

CONFEDERATION OF THE BRITISH NORTH AMERICAN PROVINCES.

═══════════

QUEBEC:
PRINTED BY HUNTER, ROSE & CO., ST. URSULE STREET.
1865.

SPEECH

ON THE

CONFEDERATION OF THE PROVINCES.

Mr. DUNKIN said—Mr. Speaker, almost every one who has yet spoken in this debate has begun with some expression of his feeling of embarrassment. For my own part, I should be glad if I could begin in some other way, but I confess that I cannot. For I certainly never did rise to address this House, or any other public body, under a feeling of such oppressive embarrassment as I experience at this moment. It is impossible for me, occupying the position in which I now stand, not to feel that I am opposed to powerful odds, and that there is a sort of foregone conclusion, here, against the views I desire. to impress upon the House. It is impossible for me not to feel that the considerations to which I have to ask the attention of the House, are so many and so complex, that no sort of justice can possibly be done them within the limits of my capacity to speak, or of yours to listen. The interests at stake, too, are so large—so much larger than ever were at stake in any question which has yet been brought under the notice of this House, and the difficulties arising out of the question are so formidable, owing in no small measure to what I must call the many reticences with which this scheme has been laid before us, and the ambiguities of expression which everywhere characterize it, as to tax seriously the courage of those who may attempt to discuss it. I feel, besides, that I am entirely cut off from that description of remark which most of all tends to make one's speech pleasant to listen to ; for I cannot prophecy smooth things, or dilate on the marvels of progress to result from Confederation in the future. There is a character of hurry, too, impressed on the whole style of this debate; everybody feels so impatient, that one can scarcely hope to express his views fully, as he would wish and ought, on this vast scheme. I have even

the feeling that my capacity for exertion is not up to its ordinary standard. I address the House in a state of health that renders me less capable than usual of physical exertions. I must, therefore, beg honorable members to make allowance for these circumstances surrounding my position; believing me that what I wish to do is to present as briefly as I can, and as truthfully as I can, my own deep seated convictions on the question now before the House. (Hear, hear.) So strongly, Mr. Speaker, do I feel my inability to discuss this scheme as I could wish, that I almost must throw myself on the forbearance of hon. members—that I hardly can help saying I should be in danger of shrinking from the duty of addressing you, but for the recollection that time and again, I have known, in cases of contest almost or quite as discouraging as this, that " the race has not been to the swift nor the battle to the strong"—that time and again I have known those who went into such contests with the best hopes of success, disappointed in their expectations. I do know, and I know that others know—I believe it to be the general conviction of those whom I address to-night, as regards this question, that whatever of popular feeling there may seem to be in favor of the views I have to combat, is anything but the deliberate result of a well-considered examination of the whole subject—is a feeling of most sudden growth, and of most passing character. (Hear, hear.) Before I go further, I may be permitted distinctly to accept the challenge, which has been more than once thrown out on the other side as to the manner in which this question ought to be discussed. I freely admit and sincerely maintain that it ought not to be discussed otherwise than as a great question, to be considered entirely on a large view of its merits. It is not a question of party, it is not a question of persons, it is not a question of merely local, or class, or passing interest, and it is not to be met by any of those passing appeals which are too often resorted to. It is not to be settled upon any ground of mere theory, or by any criticism of mere details. It requires indeed to be taken up at once as a question of principle, and also as a question of detail, involving a multitude of details; and there must necessarily be a careful criticism of such details. The question really presented is this: on the whole, viewing them collectively, are the details involved in this great scheme such as to commend the scheme itself to our approbation, or are they not? (Hear, hear.) I pledge myself that I will discuss the question from that point of view. I will do my utmost to avoid mere passing or personal allusions. I will try to tread the dangerous ground before me without arousing dangerous feelings. I do not know that I can succeed, but at least I will make the effort. This, however, I am bound to repeat at the outset, that no one can do justice to a question like this, and start with the idea of at all ignoring details. Here is a measure proposed for our acceptance, embodied in seventy-two resolutions, and which resolutions affirm a great many more than seventy-two propositions, connected with almost every principle known to have reference to the theory and practice of popular government. I say it is a scheme which is as complex and as vast as one can well imagine, and declamation about first principles can be of no real use in its discussion—can avail only to mislead in reference to it. We have to deal with no mere abstract question of a nationality, or of union or disunion, or of a Federal as opposed to a Legislative union. It is idle to talk vaguely about the maintenance of British connection, or to go into magnificent speculations about the probable results of independence, or blindly to urge this scheme as a sure preventative of annexation to the United States. These cheap and easy generalities are thoroughly unreliable. The only question is, how is this plan, in its entirety, going to work? And this question is one which is not easy to answer; it is one requiring much patience, and a close examination of details. It is the question which, if the House will lend me its attention, I will endeavor to discuss to the extent of my ability. (Hear, hear.) I may further

take leave to say at starting, that I do not approach this question from any new point of view whatever. Always I have been, and now I am, a unionist in the strictest and largest sense of the term. I desire to perpetuate the union between Upper and Lower Canada I desire to see developed, the largest union that can possibly be developed (I care not by what name you call it) between all the colonies, provinces, and dependencies of the British Crown. I desire to maintain that intimate union which ought to subsist, but which unfortunately does not subsist as it ought, between the Imperial Government and all those dependencies. I am a unionist, who especially does not desire to see the provinces of Upper and Lower Canada disunited. To my mind, this scheme does not at all present itself as one of union; and if hon. gentlemen opposite will admit the truth, they will acknowledge that, practically, it amounts to a disunion between Upper and Lower Canada. (Hear, hear.) I confess that I am irreconcileably opposed to that portion of the scheme. I repeat I do not care to see Upper and Lower Canada more dissevered than they are; on the contrary, I wish to see them brought into closer union; and far from regarding this scheme as cementing more closely the connection of these provinces with the British Empire, I look upon it as tending rather towards a not distant disunion of these provinces from the British Empire. (Hear, hear.) My position as regards this scheme is that of one who desires to see this union perpetuated, and not of one who would contemplate a state of disunion between any of the component parts of the British Empire. I hold that proper means ought to be taken to prevent our disunion from the British Empire and absorption into the United States, and that this scheme by no means tends that way. I have no fancy for democratic or republican forms or institutions, or indeed for revolutionary or political novelties of any sort. The phrase of "political creation" is no phrase of mine. I hold that the power to create is as much a higher attribute than belongs to man, in the political world, as in any other department of the universe. All we can do is to attend to and develope the ordinary growth of our institutions; and this growth, if it is to be healthy at all, must be slow. There must be the same slow, steady change in political matters, which answers to the growth visible in the physical world. I do believe in this gradual development of our institutions, but I do not believe in any of those violent and sudden changes which have for their object the creation of something entirely new. I fear this scheme is just of the character to prevent that slow, gradual, healthy development which I would wish to see steadily carried out. If I could be astonished at anything in politics, Mr. SPEAKER, I should be astonished at the attempt which has been made by some honorable gentlemen on the Treasury benches to represent the state of the public feeling on this subject as not having that mere sudden, sensational, unreliable character which I have ascribed to it. Long forgotten expressions of individual opinion; clauses said to have formed part of bills not to be found, and not known to have been even drawn; motions threatened but never made, the small party feelings of past times, from before the days of the Canada Trade Act downwards, have been pressed into service to meet the exigencies of a hard case. Well, I shall not follow out that line of argument: it is not worth while. We all know that, from the time of the union of Canada, at all events, until very lately indeed, nothing like serious discussion of the propriety or impropriety of a Federal union, or of any union at all, of the aggregate of these British American Provinces, has ever so little occupied the public mind. I will here go back merely to 1858, when the sixth Parliament was elected, and from that time bring under review, as rapidly as I can, such few points of our political history as are relevant to shew that this is the fact; although, indeed, argument to establish it is scarcely necessary. At the election of 1857–'58, what really were the issues before the country? They can be easily stated. I take the résumé, in fact, from the announcements of the Globe, the organ of the great popular party of Upper Canada at that time; mentioning not everything, but everything at all material. The great demand of the then Upper Canada Opposition, which gave the key-note to the whole political controversies of the time, was representation according to population, irrespectively of the dividing line between Upper and Lower Canada. That was urged as involving everything. It was urged for the sake of all the rest, and as sure to bring about all the rest, that was demanded by the party. It was to enable them to carry out

their opposition to what were called sectarian grants, their opposition to the holding of land in mortmain for sectarian uses, their opposition to separate schools on a sectarian basis. It was urged for the avowed purpose of obtaining uniform legislation in the future for the two sections of the province, and also what was spoken of as the assimilation of the existing institutions of the two sections of the province, but which was meant to be an assimilation of those of Lower Canada to those of Upper Canada much more than of those of Upper Canada to those of Lower Canada. (Hear, hear.) It was urged with the view of obtaining what was called free-trade, that is, an anti-Lower Canadian commercial policy. It was urged with the view of obtaining the settlement of the North-West; in other words, the relative aggrandizement of Upper Canada. It was urged, also, no doubt, with the view of obtaining what was called administrative reform—the driving from power of a set of men who were alleged, for various reasons, to be unworthy of holding it. But the great questions of measures above alluded to came first; those as to the mere men, second. (Hear, hear.) The grand object was declared to be to obtain an Upper Canadian preponderance of representation on the floor of this House, in order to put an end to everything like sectarian grants, the holding of lands in mortmain and separate schools, to render uniform our legislation, to assimilate our institutions, to carry out an anti-Lower Canadian commercial policy, and to secure the North-West for the aggrandizement of Upper Canada. In this way the question of Upper Canada against Lower Canada was unmistakably raised What must have been, what could not fail to be, the result of an appeal of that kind? It was easy to foresee that there would be returned in Upper Canada a majority in favor of these demands, and in Lower Canada an overwhelming majority against them. I do not go into this to raise the ghost of past animosities; I am merely showing what cannot be denied—that no one at that time spoke of or cared for this magnificent idea of the union of the provinces, by Confederation or otherwise. (Hear, hear.) The session commenced. Those who had the advantage or disadvantage of sitting in that Parliament that session will remember the tremendous contrast there was between all those debates which had reference to this class of subjects, and the one single debate which was attempted, but could not be made to take place, on the question of the Confederation of the Provinces. With all his ability—and there are few abler men than the hon. gentleman who undertook at that time to bring that question before the House—with all his ability, and the most earnest effort on his part to press it on the attention of the House, he could scarcely obtain a hearing. No one cared for the matter ; and it was felt by every one that such was the case. Soon after, a ministerial crisis took place. A new government came in for a few hours, and started a policy. But that policy, again, was not this policy. It did not touch this question. (Hear, hear.) It was proposed, indeed, to deal with that question of representation by population by applying some system of checks or guarantees, doing or trying to do something that might lessen the objection of Lower Canada to a change urged forward as that had been. But that was all. That government fell—fell instantly—and another was formed in its place. And the present Finance Minister, the honorable member for Sherbrooke, who, with all his ability, had not been able to obtain a serious hearing for his proposal of Confederation of the provinces, going into the new government, induced his colleagues to come before the House and the country, with that as a professed portion of their policy. I may be pardoned, perhaps, for a single word here of personal reference, for saying, en passant, that when that idea was thus broached (as it was by a Government of which I was as firm a supporter as any man in the House), I did not fail to make it known, that if ever it should be presented to the House as a practical measure by that Government, I should cease to be (so far as it was concerned) one of such supporters. (Hear, hear.) That was not the first time I had thought of it. It had long before been a matter of study with me ; and all the anxious reflection I have ever been able to give it, has only had the result of strengthening my convictions against it every day. But how was this idea then brought forward ? Tentatively, and just to neutralize the scheme which the BROWN-DORION Administration had hinted to the country. The one fire was to burn out another's burning. (Hear, hear.) The plan of that Government was to make propositions to he Imperial Government and to the gov-

ernments of the Lower Provinces. But how ? If you want to gain an object, you put that object before those to whom you propose it in the way most likely to induce them to say yes. This scheme was suggested to the Imperial Government, and to the people and governments of the Lower Provinces, precisely in the way most calculated to induce them to say no. We went and told them, "We are in such a state of embarrassment, we have political questions which so trouble and bother us, that we do not know if we can get along at all, unless you will be so kind as to come into this union with us." (Hear, hear.) It was just as though I were in business, and went round to half a dozen capitalists, telling them, " I have got into debt ; my business is gone to the dogs ; I have no business capacity ; help me by going into partnership with me, or I am ruined." (Hear, hear) If the object had been not to carry it, it does appear to me that those gentlemen could not have taken a better method of accomplishing that object. And we saw this—that just so soon as it was found that the Lower Provinces did not, as under the circumstances they could not, say yes to a proposal of this kind, and that the Imperial Government let the matter drop, our Administration let it drop too. We never heard another word about it The despatches were laid on our table in 1859, but nobody asked a question about them. The child was still-born, and no one troubled himself about its want of baptism. We went on with our old questions—representation by population ; Upper Canada against Lower Canada ; measures, to a great extent ; men also, to a great and increasing extent. And we quarrelled and fought about almost everything, but did not waste a thought or word upon this gigantic question of the Confederation of these provinces. (Hear, hear.) In a little while we drifted into another crisis—that of 1862. And from the time of that crisis, and the formation of the MACDONALD-SICOTTE Administration, down to the time when the present Administration was, last summer, brought into its present shape, the one prominent demand made upon political parties and political men everywhere was, to set aside the older questions of measures, and occupy ourselves very much more—not to say exclusively—with the question of men. (Hear, hear.) I am not blaming honorable gentlemen; I am not raising the question whether they were right or wrong in taking that course. They may have been the purest patriots, the most farseeing statesmen the world has known, for ought I care. What I say is merely this, that whether for good or evil, whether wisely or unwisely, the fact is, that the public mind was not occupied in the least with this Confederation question. After having fought a long time, mainly about measures, and secondarily about men, we were all suddenly called upon, in 1862, to consider nothing but the question of the men who were to do everything right, and to settle everything fairly and honestly, and so forth. Representation by population was unmistakably, for a time at least, laid upon the shelf, declared to be secondary, almost unimportant. It had been half shelved some time before; then, it was wholly shelved. It was hardly taken down from the shelf in 1863, when the MACDONALD-DORION Government merely put it back to the same place, which it had long occupied to no purpose of a practical character under the CARTIER-MACDONALD Administration. (Hear, hear.) Such, then, was the state of affairs—nobody thinking or caring about this great question, until last Session of Parliament, when the hon. member for South Oxford, the present President of the Council, moved for and obtained a committee on the subject of constitutional changes generally. Certainly that hon. gentleman did a very clever thing, in embodying in his motion extracts from the unfortunate defunct dispatch of Messrs. CARTIER, GALT and ROSS.

HON. ATTY. GEN. CARTIER—It was a fortunate despatch—unfortunate for you, but fortunate for us.

MR. DUNKIN—It is an old proverb that says "He laughs well who laughs last."

HON. ATTY. GEN. CARTIER—I expect to laugh the last.

MR. DUNKIN—No doubt. But I do not care to joke in a matter which I think of a very serious character; and, seriously speaking, I think the hon. gentleman is very wrong. We have yet to see, in the first place, whether the thing is done, and then, if it is done, whether it succeeds.

HON. MR. McGEE—"If 'twere done, 'twere well 'twere done quickly."

MR. DUNKIN—The Minister of Agriculture is too good a Shakspearian to need to be reminded that the thing to be done in that case was a something very bad. The hon. gentleman is welcome to all he can make of his quotation,—"If 'twere done when 'tis done, then 'twere well it were done quickly." To return, however. It was clever, undoubtedly clever, in the hon. member for South Oxford to quote from the despatch of these hon. gentlemen—then, by the way, in opposition to the then Government and to himself —an expression of opinion almost coinciding with his own. He carried his committee. No one made any great objection to it. I have been told that I am guilty of some sort of inconsistency, after having voted for that committee, in now opposing this measure. The *sequitur* is hard to see. I did certainly speak and vote for it, but on the express ground that I believed it would do no sort of harm, and that, on the contrary, it might have the good effect of leading other hon. gentlemen to the sober conclusion at which I had long before arrived myself. I therefore had no objection to the committee, and I sat on it. I am not going to reveal what have been called the secrets of the committee. As in many other like cases, there was mighty little in them. Owing to accidents, wholly aside from this question of Confederation, the report of the committee was presented on the very night that vote happened to be given, indirectly adverse to the TACHE-MACDONALD Administration. The report itself was an accident. All the allusion there was in it to Federation of any sort, found its way there at the last moment and unexpectedly. It is no violation of confidence to say that it was even voted against by the leader of this House, the Attorney General for Upper Canada, the now leading advocate of the present scheme. That fact is on the printed record. It was voted against, also, by the members for Cornwall and West Elgin. There were five other members, of whom I am sorry I was one, who were absent; had I been there, unquestionably my vote would have been against it. (Hear, hear.) And, Mr. SPEAKER, those who were in this House at the time that report was made, will remember pretty well the more than cool indifference with which it was here received, little or nothing, after all, as it amounted to. Well, this vote in the House thus following, the opportunity suddenly offered to honorable gentlemen opposite of starting on a tack which, up to that moment, I believe no two men in the House had ever thought of as possible. And from that day to this, a series of accidents, each one more extraordinary than its predecessor, has led to a state of things about as extraordinary as the accidents themselves were. (Laughter.)

Hon. Atty. Gen. CARTIER—It is said the world was made by a series of accidents.

Mr. DUNKIN—I dare say some people think so ; and it may be so according to the theology of my hon. friend, but not according to mine. I repeat, what has happened since has been tolerably unexpected, even by the actors in those occurrences. I do not believe they were expected by anybody; and none, I fancy, have been more surprised at them than the very men who now take all the advantage possible of them, and even the credit of having brought them about. And how, Mr. SPEAKER, was this scheme presented to the public ? Piecemeal, and with reticences innumerable ; in a way that made it hardly possible to criticise it in any of its parts. When, after several members of the Government of this province and several other members of the Conference had gone into long explanations of it publicly at Quebec, Montreal and Toronto, the honorable member for Hochelaga came out with a criticism upon and a dissent from it. He was set upon with a clamor, to the effect that he ought not to have pronounced himself so soon, as the whole scheme was not yet developed ! It was said he had misrepresented the scheme, and ought to have waited until its details were really known before attacking it. Brought thus before the country, in piecemeal style, with some portions kept back, and others ambiguously and even contradictorily stated, no one could seriously take hold of it. After some time, it is true, a printed paper, purporting to set forth the resolutions of the Conference, was sent round to members, but with the word "Private" written on it, as much as to say that it was not officially communicated, and must be made no public use of. That that private communication was not even perfectly accurate, is now perfectly well known ; but that was of little consequence, as it could not be made use of publicly. Such is the way in which this matter was laid before the people. Every possible advantage was given to the people to praise it from every point of view, and nobody got a fair opportunity of saying that he did not like it. The praise was carefully prepared and published, and everything that could possibly be done to prepare the public mind for the scheme before it final announce-

ment was skilfully done. And now what have we ? Why, the cry that the whole thing must be passed, "now or never." It will never pass, we are told, if it does not pass now ! (Hear, hear.) Was there ever a measure of this magnitude before, on which the heart of a country was set, the whole of which was so wise and good as this scheme is said to be—and yet, that had to be passed (the whole of it) at once, or never ? (Hear, hear.) We are even told that it is a positive treaty— made however, by the way, by parties who were never authorized to make any treaty at all. I must say, for one, that I cannot but see in all this precipitancy the unmistakeable admission de facto, that the Government themselves know and feel that the feeling they have got up in favor of this scheme is a passing feeling of momentary duration, that they cannot themselves in the least rely upon. (Hear, hear.) Mr. SPEAKER, it is rather curious that hon. gentlemen, in recommending this scheme of theirs, seem never to be tired of speaking of its excellencies in general, and of modestly eulogizing the wisdom, and foresight, and statesmanship of those who got it up. I cannot wonder that their judgment in this behalf should be a little led astray by their surprise at the success which has so far attended their project. Their "officious" visit to Prince Edward Island took but a very few days, and it resulted in the scheme of a legislative union for the Lower Provinces being (as I think, unfortunately) laid aside ; and then followed the Conference at Quebec, where these twelve honorable gentlemen representing Canada, and twenty-one other gentlemen representing the Lower Provinces, sat together for the long period of nineteen days—seventeen working days and two Sundays—and as the result of these seventeen days of but partial work by the way, we have from these thirty-three gentlemen a scheme of a Constitution which they vaunt of as being altogether better than that of the model republic of the United States, and even than that of the model kingdom of Great Britain. Neither the model republic nor yet the model kingdom of whose glorious traditions and associations we are all so proud, is for a moment to be compared with this work of theirs. (Hear, hear.) So perfect do they seem to regard their pet measure, that they tell us we must not take time to discuss it. Even though Her Majesty's Secretary of State has told us that there are features of it that require further consideration and must be revised, yet they tell us that we must not change a letter or line of it. (Hear, hear.) And yet, we are at the same time told that the details of this scheme, if examined at all, must be examined and viewed as those of a compromise. It is not, they freely admit, as satisfactory in its details as any of us would desire to have; but it is all we can get, and must be accepted or rejected as a whole. It must be examined in the very spirit of compromise, meaning that no serious fault shall be found with it, however unsatisfactory it may be I have heard of Paddy's notion of a reciprocity that was all on one side.

Hon. Mr. McGEE—Now let us have no national reflections. (Laughter.)

Mr. DUNKIN—Oh! I mean it as a national compliment. I would, however, ask hon. gentlemen opposite not to throw across the House these jokes; not that I object to an occasional interruption by way of question, but mere jokes thrown into the discussion of a serious subject do not help any man who desires to present his honest, sincere and serious views on a grave question. I must ask the two hon. members of the Government, who have several times, by means of interruptions of that nature, tried to throw me off the track, to desist from such course in future.

Hon. Atty. Gen. CARTIER—I am sure the hon. gentleman did not intend to disconcert you, nor had I any such purpose in view.

Mr. DUNKIN—I will not say it is done for that purpose; but I feel myself more than usually annoyed with interruptions tonight, because the subject is of a nature to require the closest attention. This measure, then, it is said, must be examined in this spirit of compromise, that is to say, not objecting to any of its provisions. One of the expressions used by the hon. gentleman was—that we should not require in the scheme "an impossible perfection." Well, sir, I do not think there is any danger of our finding any impossible perfection in it, or anything relating to it, unless, indeed, in one particular direction; and in that direction I do not know but that there has been attained all possible perfection at least, if not an impossible perfection. I allude to that particular kind of wisdom and foresight which marks the astute official politician, as contradistinguished from the far-seeing statesman. (Hear, hear.) There has been exhibited, in this one respect, an all but impossible perfection. Every feeling, every

interest, every class, is bid for in the cleverest way imaginable. The seat of the Federal Government is to be at Ottawa, of course. The Governor General or other head of this magnificent future vice-royalty, or what not, will hold his court and parliament at Ottawa; but a handsome sop is thrown to Quebec and Toronto, also. They, too, are each to have a provincial court and legislature and governmental departments. Everything for everybody! As to the state that is to be created, its style and rank are left in most delightful ambiguity. We may be honored with the dignity of a kingdom, or of a vice-royalty, or of we know not what. All we are assured of is, that it is to be a something better, higher and more grand than we now have. Perhaps the Sovereign herself will occasionally come over and exercise her authority in person; or, perhaps, a throne will be created for some member of the royal family; or, failing such dreams as these, we are told, at the least, in reference to the character of the representative who is to be sent here in place of the Sovereign—that is to say. the representative who is to administer the government during the ordinary absence of the Sovereign from this part of the British dominions—we are told, I say, by the leader of this House, that, in view of the functions to be entrusted to him, the high position he is to hold, the vice-regal state he will have to keep, it is possible we shall, at least, have sent out here in that capacity, hereafter, men of the class emphatically called statesmen. I have no taste for paying what may be termed courtier compliments to the living; but, looking back only to the dead, of whom one may speak freely, without such fear, I must say that those who have been appointed to administer our government in the past are hardly of the class to be looked down upon—that the list in which we find the names of Durham, Sydenham, Metcalfe, and Elgin, is not precisely a list of men inferior to the higher class of those whom we call statesmen; and I am not quite sure that even after this great Confederacy shall have been established, men of much higher mark than those we have already had will be appointed to rule over it. Be that as it may, however, the bait is thrown out that we are to have men much higher than we ever had before; that in all manner of ways our state is to be better, finer, grander, in fact, than our imagination can well conceive. (Laughter.) We are, it seems, among other things, to get a little more than we now have of what is called a feature of the British Constitution, in the composition of the Legislative Council. It has been spoken of as an impropriety, almost treasonable, to hint at it as a bait thrown out to gentlemen who have been elected to the Legislative Council for a fixed period, that by voting for this scheme they may get themselves made legislative councillors for life. If in this scheme provision had been made, in regard to the members of this branch of the Legislature, that they should hold their seats, not for life, but say, for a mere period of five years, I rather think there would be few found here very mealy-mouthed on the subject; and when it is offered to men who, like ourselves, will have to go before their constituents within a few months, or years, at most, that they are to be made legislative councillors for life, the bait, I think, is not a very small one. (Hear, hear.) We are told, too, on the face of this scheme, that the choice is to be made by the present governments of the several provinces; but of course with perfect fairness to the Opposition in each province! Most satisfactory! Each Opposition is to be treated with perfect fairness —"it is so nominated in the bond." We hear of a minister of the Crown in one place, addressing his neighbors, and telling them they may depend on it, that when Her Majesty comes to make the selection, the utmost respect will be paid to the rights and privileges of the elected members, so that their elected member will have the fairest chance of becoming a life member of the Confederate Legislative Council. In another place, on the other hand, we hear from another minister of the Crown that those gentlemen who hold patents of appointment for life may feel quite as safe, for certainly their claim to be retained in their present position is sure to have full weight. Further, in Lower Canada, each locality is told that it may rest satisfied it will not be overlooked, for each is to be represented in the Legislative Council by a gentleman residing or holding property in it; and both origins and both creeds alike are thus to have representation and full protection. Another point upon which there has been a like pleasant sort of ambiguity kept up, is as to who are to make the future nominations to this Legislative Council. Viewing this part of the scheme as a matter of principle, one would have thought that these future nominations must be made on the

Federal principle. It was not expressly so stated; it is not (as we are at last here told) it is not so meant; but till we were so told, everybody who thought one way said that the resolutions meant it to be that way, and all who thought the other way conveniently found the resolutions to justify their way of thinking. Well, turning then to matters which affect this House, the same sort of thing is still observable. Representation by population is given to meet the grand demand of Upper Canada; but the people of Lower Canada are assured, in the same breath, that it will not hurt them; that their institutions and privileges are made perfectly safe; that they will even have as many members in the Lower House as before, and that they will, in a variety of ways, be really better off than ever. A delightful ambiguity is found, too, upon the point as to who will make the future apportionments of the constituencies. The leader of the Government, in explaining the scheme the other night, admitted that the decennial revisions of our representation districts are really not to be left to the local legislatures, but are to be dealt with altogether by the Federal Legislature. Till then most people, I believe, had held the contrary; but all had admitted the text of the resolutions to be equivocal, and each party had of course interpreted them as it wished. The postponement of the local constitutions is of the same character. Everyone is given to understand that the thing will be made to work to the satisfaction of all; each is promised that he shall have it as he wants. Those who hold to the principle of responsible government, as commonly understood, in the local administrations are, of course, told to expect a lieutenant-governor, with a cabinet, and, presumably, two branches of a local legislature. Those who would have two legislative bodies, without a responsible ministry, are told that very well it may be so. Whoever prefers one legislative body, hears that it is beyond a doubt there very well may only be one; and those again who, even with one House, do not wish to see responsible government in the provinces, are assured that the machinery is likely to be very simple; that each province will probably have a lieutenant-governor, with a few heads of needed departments, and one House, and that so, no doubt, the affairs of each province can be managed most economically and to the entire satisfaction of all. The appointment of lieutenant-governors is again a bait, and perhaps not a small one for more than a few of our public men. The power of disallowance of local bills, and also that of reserving them for the sanction of the General Government, are on the one hand represented as realities—powers that will really be exercised by the General Government to restrain improper local legislation—to make everything safe for those who want a Legislative rather than a Federal union; but on the other hand, to those who do not want a legislative union, it is represented that they mean nothing at all, and will never be exercised. (Hear, hear.) Uniformity of laws again is to be given to all the provinces, if they desire it, except Lower Canada; but by a peculiar provision of the Constitution, although nothing can be done by the General Parliament to render the laws uniform, without the consent of the provinces concerned, it is stipulated that it shall be impossible for Lower Canada, even though she should desire it, to have her laws uniform with those of the other provinces. So, too, with regard to education in Upper and Lower Canada; the provision is to be made, no one knows how, for everybody, and all are guaranteed some sort of satisfaction. It is true we are not told what the promised measures on this head are to be; whether they really will give increased facilities to the minorities in the two sections for the education of their youth in their own way or not; but we are to take the promise as all right, and everybody is required to be content. Turning to the financial features of the scheme, we find it roundly stated that all the debts and liabilities of each province are to be assumed by the General Government; but if we look again into details we find that—no, they are not. There is a something here, too, beyond what appears on the face of things. Upper and Lower Canada are each to stay burthened with some unstated parts of the debt of Canada, and the other provinces are to have *bonuses* of unstated and variant amounts, not easy to be come at The financial portion of the scheme, equally with every other, is presented to everybody in whatever light he would like to view it in. It will surely bring about economy, because the local governments will have so little to expend unless they resort to direct taxation; but yet, on the other hand, it is as surely to carry us through all sorts of wild expenditure—to give us new and exhaustless credit

in England—to make possible vast defensive works throughout the country—to construct the Intercolonial Railway—to enlarge our canals westward—to create no one knows how vast a scheme of communication with the far North-West. Literally, it sounds at every turn as a promise of everything for everybody; and yet, when each comes to ask how much it promises, and how, and where, and when, the whole is to be found ambiguous, unsubstantial and unreal. (Hear, hear.). I repeat, there is everywhere throughout this scheme a most amazing amount of that sort of cleverness which may characterize the astute politician, but which, I think, I shall be able to show is yet far from being the wisdom and foresight characteristic of the far-seeing statesman. (Hear, hear.) The game of all things to all men is a game that cannot be played with success in the long run. It can, under any circumstances, be but temporary in its success. (Hear, hear.) Seriously, then, Mr. SPEAKER, I pass on to examine this work in a constitutional point of view, clearing away, as best one may, these ambiguities that surround it, dealing with it as it is, and comparing it primarily with the Constitution of the United States, and secondarily with the Constitution of Great Britain. I wish I could compare it primarily with that of Great Britain; but it is so much more like that of the United States, that I cannot. In parts only has it any resemblance to the British Constitution; and for this reason the order of comparison cannot be reversed. I must say, before I go further, that I am by no means an admirer of a great deal that I find in the Constitution of the United States. I have always preferred, decidedly preferred, and do now prefer, our own British Constitution. But this, at least, no one can deny, that the framers of the American Constitution were great men, wise men, far-seeing men; that their work was a great work; and that to compare anybody else's work—especially a work such as this, of the few gentlemen, doubtless able gentlemen, who framed this Constitution—with it, is to submit that work to a very severe and trying test. (Hear, hear.) The framers of the Constitution of the United States were, indeed, great men—living in, and the product of a great age, who had passed through a great ordeal and been brought up to the level of their work by great events in which they had been leading actors; and their work was a great work, which cost much time and much

discussion, and underwent long and pains-
taking revision of all sorts, in all quarters,
before it was finally adopted. (Hear, hear.)
Yet we are called upon to admit now, and to
admit it without examination, that this work
of thirty-three gentlemen, done in seventeen
days, is a much better work than that; and
not only so, but that it is even better for
our people and situation, than the time-
honored Constitution of our Mother Land;
that it combines essentially the advantages
of both, with the disadvantages of neither.
I do not think so. The Constitution of the
United States, it must be borne in mind, at
least lasted seventy years without fracture.
It has stood a good deal of straining, from
events beyond the possible foresight or control of those who framed it; and it may yet
stand many more years, notwithstanding
this late strain upon it. If, indeed, Louisiana
had not been purchased, if the cotton-gin
had not been invented—the two unforeseen
events which so encouraged the growth
of cotton and therefore of slavery—if it
had not been for these, what I may call
extraneous events, which could not be
expected to enter into the minds of the
framers of that Constitution, it probably
would not have received the shock · that
it has received; but we do not know yet
that that shock will have a fatal effect,
or that it will break up the wonderful fabric
which they created. Perhaps it may change
that fabric more or less in some of its parts;
and after it shall have passed away, the fabric
itself may not improbably endure for a very
long time to come. But as to this proposed
Constitution of ours, should it become the
organic law of the land, how long will it last?
How will it work, if it does last? And to
or towards what, while working, will it tend?
To these questions, I have now to call the
earnest attention of this House. I begin,
Mr. SPEAKER, with the future House of
Commons—falsely so called. I shall not take
up the different resolutions one after another,
and criticize them in that manner; but I
will take up the different leading features of
the scheme consecutively, and endeavor not
to misrepresent them. If I should do so,
or at all misstate their character or probable
effects, I give honorable gentlemen opposite
full leave, if only they will do so without
throwing jokes across the floor of the House,
to correct me, and I will do my best to set
myself right. The House of Commons,
then, incorrectly so called, to distinguish it

from the other House that corresponds
with, but is not named after the House
of Lords, the Legislative Council, forms
the leading feature of this project; and
I take it up first, comparing it with the
House of Representatives of the United
States, and speaking here not so much of its
powers as of its composition. I cannot, in
this view, compare it with the Imperial
House of Commons, because the principle of
its construction is so entirely different. In
that respect, it is simply copied from what I
think the wrong model; and the copied
parts correspond most faithfully and exactly
with what I venture to call the least desirable
features of the Constitution of the United
States House of Representatives. (Hear,
hear.) The copy is not, I repeat, of a thing
absolutely good, but only of a thing as good
as the framers of the Constitution of the
United States, circumstanced as they were,
could make it; but the peculiarity of their
system that I object to, was not at all necessary to ours. I think it was absolutely
unnecessary; I think it even very much of
an excrescence. It can hardly be denied,
Mr. SPEAKER, that there is a good deal of
practical objection to the plan of shifting
representation districts, which is what this
system adopts, and what the system of the
United States adopted. Every ten years the
representation from each province in the
House of Commons is to be changed or
readjusted by a rule which, for all practical
purposes, is essentially the same as that of
the United States. Of course we have not
the little addition of the allowance for the
three-fifths of the slave population which
they have; but decennially we are to take
the population of the several provinces, and
by a rule in all essentials common to the
two systems, we are to declare how many
representation districts are to be allowed to
each province. Now, the result of that
system must be that we can have no lasting
constituencies for the future House of Commons. These representation districts cannot
be kept to correspond with our municipal,
business or registration districts, or with our
districts for representation in our provincial
legislatures. We are to have a set of special,
shifting districts for the mere purpose of
electing our Federal House of Commons. I
must say that this principle is not, from a British point of view, a sound one. (Hear, hear.)
What we ought to do is, to try to establish
in this country of ours a set of representation

districts as permanent and as closely coinciding with our territorial divisions existing for other purposes, as circumstances will allow us to have them; subdividing or otherwise altering them, or erecting new ones, only as occasion may be found to require.

Hon. Att'y. Gen. CARTIER—We will do that for the local parliaments.

Mr. DUNKIN—Perhaps so, and perhaps not. That distinction, however, is just what I complain of. We are to change our districts for purposes of representation in the local parliaments, if we like, but not unless we like. These subdivisions of our provinces may thus, in the main, be permanent. But for representation in the Federal Parliament we are, at each of these decennial periods, to have a general readjustment of the whole country, so as to divide each province anew into its due number of aliquot parts. This is an innovation on our usages, greatly for the worse. It goes to destroy that character of reality, convenience and stability which—if our system, as a whole, is to have such character—had need be maintained to the utmost extent practicable, in respect of our constituencies and of our minor territorial delimitations generally. This changing every ten years brings together electors who have not been in the habit of acting with each other. In England they do nothing of this sort; they do not change their limits lightly. The several bodies of men who send representatives to the Imperial House of Commons have the habit of so coming together, as bodies not likely to be broken up. We ought to keep this as an element of our Constitution, but it is carefully eliminated from it.

Hon. Mr. McDOUGALL—I am sure the honorable gentleman does not wish to build up an argument on a misconception of the resolutions for the purpose of misrepresentation. I am sure that he must have observed this fact, that it may, and probably will often happen, that there will be no change as to the number of members or electoral districts, and there certainly will be none if the increase of population in Lower Canada keeps pace with that in Upper Canada, and therefore the evil he complains of will not occur unless there be some different rule of increase from that which has prevailed heretofore.

Mr. DUNKIN—If any one imagines that the population of the different provinces is going to increase upon any thing like the same rule, then I differ from him. I believe there will be a very much more rapid rate of increase in some provinces than in others; a divergence between them in this respect, of the same kind, and perhaps, even to the same degree as in the case of the United States. There, in the old states, at every decennial revision, the number of representatives lessens, and in the new states it increases, and that rapidly. It is only in the comparatively few states which may be said to be neither old nor new that it remains about the same. The rule is one of change, for the country everywhere. Any escape from change is the exception. And with us, those provinces which shall be found to increase faster than Lower Canada, as some certainly will be, will re-divide their whole territory every ten years, in order to increase their number of districts; and those which increase slower will do the same, in order to cut some off. Even Lower Canada, to meet the varying rates of increase of its several parts, will be drawn into doing the same sort of thing. I shall be told, no doubt, that this need not be—that mere partial changes here and there may be made to answer the end; but I know that in the nature of things it will be, that such partial changes will not be made the rule. The sweeping rule is laid down, in the abstract, of basing representation on mere population; and that rule is sure to be followed out—not only as between the several provinces, but also as within each; and here again, not only as for Federal, but also as for provincial legislation. For all legislative purposes, we must look to have all our territorial divisions open to frequent, one might say perpetual, reconstruction; and this subject perpetually to the disturbing influences of the party warfare of the hour. The exigencies of that warfare, we may be sure, will tell; and whatever the party in the ascendant, whether in the country at large or locally, will find means in this part of our machinery for advancing its ends—means not quite of the sort to commend themselves to one's approval. (Hear, hear.) It is claimed, I know, as a merit of this scheme, that it allows a five years' term to our House of Commons, in place of the two years' term fixed for the House of Representatives. Apart from these decennial revisions, I would be glad of this. But five is the half of ten, I think; and though our Houses of Commons may often not last their full term, there will yet seldom or never, in all probability, be more than either two or three general elections held between any two decennial revisions. A less satisfactory arrangement, if one is to think of our House of Commons at all treading in the footsteps of its great namesake, I confess I can hardly imagine. There everything favors that combined steadiness and variety of local influences upon the representative machinery which is at once characteristic of, and essential to, the British system, and without which neither public parties nor public men can act or last us it requires they should. Here everything is to be allowed to tend in precisely the opposite direction. Nor is this all. At home, while the constituencies are wisely kept as lasting as they can be, the members they return are all held members of the one House of Commons, as little distinguished by the English, Scotch, Irish or Welsh location of their constituencies as they well can be. Here, again, this United States system which we are asked to copy, is the reverse, and the reverse of sound judgment. The House of Representatives is an aggregate of state delegations, and our mock House of Commons is to be an aggregate of provincial delegations. Each man is to come to it ticketed as an Upper or Lower Canadian, a New Brunswicker, a Nova Scotian, Newfoundlander, a Prince Edward Islander, or what not. These distinctions, which, if we are to be a united people, we had better try to sink, we are to keep up and exaggerate. The system will do that, and but too well. There is, however, one marked contrast as to this, between the system of the United States and that proposed here. In the United States, for the House of Representatives, the system is at least sure to work, whether for good or evil. Theirs is a true Federation. Its founders took care, when, with the foresight of statesmen, they arranged the details of their constitution, to frame it so as to work in all its important parts, and with that end they left it mainly to the several states to work out the arithmetical rule laid down for these decennial revisions, giving them such powers as to make sure that the thing intended would be really and punctually done. I thought when I read these resolutions first, that it was, of course, the intention of their framers to adopt that system here; but we are now authoritatively told that it is not so. The General Parliament is alone to do the whole work of these re-divisions of the constituencies throughout the provinces. But, suppose that for any cause, such as readily may suggest itself—under pretext of alleged incorrectness of a census, or without pretext—it should fail to discharge this duty promptly, or should discharge it in a questionable way, or not at all—what then? Is the Imperial Parliament to reserve a right of interference in such case; or is the doctrine broached the other night by the Attorney General for Lower Canada, as to its power to revoke our constitutional charters, to be acted on? I should fancy not. But why, then, pretend to ask the Imperial Parliament to do so weak a thing as to lay down for us a bad rule for all time to come, merely that we may follow it or not, as in our wisdom or unwisdom we may please? Well, then, Mr. SPEAKER, I turn next to our Legislative Council — too little like the House of Lords, to bear even a moment's comparison in that direction. It must be compared with the Senate of the United States; but the differences here are very wide. The framers of this Constitution have here contrived a system quite different from that; and when we are told (as it seems we are) that the Legislative Council is to represent especially the Federal element in our Constitution, I do not hesitate to affirm that there is not a particle of the Federal principle about it; that it is the merest sham that can be imagined. (Hear, hear.) To show the contrast. The Senate of the United States consists of just two senators, freely chosen by the Legislature of each State of the Union.

HON. ATTY. GEN. CARTIER — And sometimes by the Governor.

MR. DUNKIN—That does not in the least touch what I am saying. I say that the Senate consists of just two senators from each state, who are freely selected by the legislature of each state. It is true that in case of any casual vacancy power is given to the Governor of the state to fill up such vacancy until the next meeting of the legislature of the state. But it is the legislatures of the several states who regularly elect these senators from each, for a stated term of six years, and subject to an arrangement for their retiring in such rotation as never to leave any state unrepresented. Well, sir, the Senate of the United States, thus constituted of two picked men from each state, and presided over by the Vice-President or by one of themselves, freely chosen by themselves, have devolved upon them the important judicial function of impeachment. Even the President of the United States may be impeached before them for treason or

15

malversation in office. They have a large share of executive power also; sitting in secret session upon all treaties and upon most appointments to office, that is to say, upon all appointments of the more important kind. There are appointments which the President may make without their concurrence; but as a rule, there are no important appointments which he can so make. Every treaty and every important appointment must go before them, and may be disallowed by them. They further exercise coördinate legislative functions, as to expenditure and taxation, with the House of Representatives. From all these circumstances combined, the Senate of the United States is, I believe, on the whole, the ablest deliberative body the world has ever known. As to men of third and fourth rate importance finding their way there, it is hardly possible. The members of the Senate, almost without exception, are first or second-rate men. There are no small men among them. (Cries of "Yes! yes!") Well, Mr. SPEAKER, there is certainly no proportion of small men, comparatively speaking.

HON. ATTY. GEN. CARTIER—It is a question at this moment as to the relative averages of the House of Representatives and of the Senate. I heard it discussed when I was in Washington.

HON. MR. HOLTON—Hear! hear!! Looking to Washington. (Laughter.)

MR. DUNKIN—What I say is, I believe, fully borne out by constitutional writers of the highest mark—by DE TOCQUEVILLE, CHEVALIER, and others. They say that the peculiar constitution and attributes of the Senate of the United States have made it a deliberative body of the very highest mark. And even were it doubtful whether or not in this respect it is all I have called it, at least of this there can be no doubt at all. As intended for the Federal check in the system of the United States, it is a machine simply perfect. It is a very able, deliberative body, of moderate numbers, carefully chosen on the strictest principle of federation, changing constantly, and having, on every matter of importance, a voice and veto of the most efficient kind. For stopping everything, for bringing about a deadlock—all parts of their machinery viewed together—it affords no formidable facilities; whilst for preventing anything from being done which it may be to the public interest, or to that of any number of the states, to prevent, it is as perfect as can be. Look now on the other hand, Mr. SPEAKER, at the Legislative Council under the proposed Confederation; what is it? There is a sort of attempt to prevent its numbers from resting on a population basis; and this is about the only principle I can find in it. (Hear, hear.) It would seem to have been thought, that as the branch of the legislature was to be shared between the provinces in the ratio of their population, there must be some other rule followed for the Upper Chamber. So we are to have twenty-four for Upper Canada, twenty-four for Lower Canada, twenty-four for the three Lower Provinces, and four for Newfoundland; simply, I suppose, because the populations of these equalized sections are not equal, and because four is not in proportion to the population of Newfoundland. (Hear, hear.) And these legislative councillors, thus limited in number, are to hold their seats for life. They are not to be even freely chosen, in the first instance, at least, from the principal men in each section of the country. They are to be selected, as far as possible, from the small number of gentlemen holding seats in the present Legislative Council, either by the accident of their having been nominated to them some time ago, or by the chances of popular election since; and until that panel is exhausted, no other person in any province is to be taken; and hereafter, Mr. SPEAKER, as vacancies occur, they are to be filled as we are now told —and this is the strangest thing of all—not by the provincial legislatures, nor by any authority or under any avowed influence of the local kind, but possibly by the General Government. And forsooth, this is called the Federal feature of our system! (Hear, hear.) The vacancies, to be sure, in Lower Canada are to be filled by selection of individuals having or holding property in Lower Canada,—and more than that, in particular territorial divisions of Lower Canada! But are these individuals to be ever so little chosen by the people of such territorial divisions, or even of Lower Canada, or with any necessary reference to their wishes in that behalf? Bless you, no! not at all. That would go towards making a Federal body of this House! (Hear, hear.) It might then be something of a Federal check upon the General Government, and that would never do. But suppose this should happen—and honourable gentlemen opposite must admit that it may,—that in the Federal Executive Council some one province or other—Upper Canada, Lower Canada, or any other, no matter which— either is not represented, or is represented otherwise than as it would wish to be. While thus out in the cold, a vacancy arises in the Legislative Council, requiring to be filled as for such province. Where is the guarantee that it will be filled on any sort of Federal principle? (Hear, hear.) And yet, what worse wrong or insult could be put upon a province, than would be involved in the kind of selection likely under such circumstances to be made for it? Surely, Mr. SPEAKER, this Legislative Council, constituted so differently from the Senate of the United States, presided over by a functionary to be nominated by the General Government; having no such functions of a judicial or executive character as attached to that body, and cut off from that minute oversight of the finances which attaches to the Senate of the United States; although it may be a first-rate deadlock; although it may be able to interpose an absolute veto, for no one can say how long, on all legislation, would be no Federal check at all. I believe it to be a very near approach to the worst system which could be devised in legislation. While the Senate of the United States is nearly perfect in the one way, our Legislative Council is to be as nearly perfect in the other way. (Laughter.) The Hon. Attorney General for Upper Canada, the other night, devised and stated just the cleverest defence he could, of this constitution of the Legislative Council. But what did it amount to? Nothing. He undertook to tell us, that from the ordinary course of events, the deaths to be counted on in a body numbering its certain proportion of elderly men, and so forth, the personal composition of this Council would not change so slowly as many feared. He also urged that those who thus found their way into it would be but men after all—perhaps politicians a little or more than a little given to complaisance—but at any rate men, who would know they had no great personal hold on public confidence; and so, that they might sometimes even yield to pressure too easily, in place of resisting it too much. Well, sir, I have heard it said that every government in the world is in a certain sense a constitutional government—a government, that is to say, tempered by check of some kind. The despotism of the Grand Turk has been said to have its constitutional check in a salutary fear of the bow-string; and there may prove to be something of the same sort here. But I confess I do not like the quasi-despotism of this Legislative Council, even though so tempered. Representing no public opinion or real power of any kind, it may hurt the less;

but it can never tend to good, and it can never last. It is satisfactory for one to find that in this view I do not stand alone. This plan is condemned, not simply by the Colonial Secretary, but by the Imperial Government, as one which cannot be carried out. The Imperial authorities cannot but see that a body appointed for life and limited in numbers, is just the worst body that could be contrived—ridiculously the worst.

HON. ATTY. GEN. CARTIER—Do they say it is the worst?

MR. DUNKIN—I say it is the worst. They say it is bad. It is condemned by Her Majesty's Government, in diplomatic terms it may be, but in sufficiently emphatic terms. I believe Her Majesty's Government regard it as I do—as pretty nonsensical. I know it may be said that Her Majesty's Government, perhaps, may apply a remedy by leaving out the provision about a limited number of members.

HON. ATTY. GEN. CARTIER—That is our security.

MR. DUNKIN—Security it is none, but the very contrary. But, Mr. SPEAKER, even though this should be done, or though the Imperial Act should even not state the restrictions by which it is proposed to limit the Crown in its first choice of Legislative Councillors, such remedy would be the merest palliative imaginable. The restrictions on such choice would be maintained in practice all the same; and even the limitations as to number would remain as an understood rule, to be set aside for no cause, much less grave than might suffice to sweep away even a clause of an act of the Imperial Parliament. Before leaving this subject, Mr. SPEAKER, let me ask the attention of the House for a few moments to the past history of Canada in respect of our Legislative Council. (Hear, hear.) Did it not happen, as matter of fact, that the first Legislative Council of Canada, not being limited in point of numbers, being like the House of Lords in that respect—the Crown, I say, having the full choice of its members, and full control over their number—did it not happen, I say, that its members were most of them, for some time, named from one side in politics? The gentlemen named by Lord SYDENHAM and his immediate successors, were, undoubtedly, most respectable. There was nothing out of common course that I see about these appointments; they were party, political appointments of the ordinary kind. And under this proposed scheme the same kind of thing would naturally happen again.

But in 1848, with a change of government, it became necessary to carry through Parliament a measure or measures to which it was well known that a large majority of this Upper House were decidedly opposed. There had to be some talking about a swamping of the House —a similar step to what was threatened once in the constitutional history of Great Britain. It was not really done. It did not need to be done, or at least, it only needed to be done in part; the peculiarity of the position of honorable gentlemen, and the impossibility of their standing out beyond a certain point, made it unnecessary to carry out the threat to extremity. But it was carried far enough to destroy their self-respect, and the respect of the public for them. It was felt that they had no sufficient *status* in the country; they sank in public opinion, and sank and sank until every one quietly acquiesced in the change which was afterwards made in the Constitution of the Council. (Hear, hear.) I do not overstate the truth when I say that the Legislative Council so sank in public opinion, because there was no machinery by which public opinion could act upon it, except that of a further creation of councillors by the Crown, and there being no other way of averting a deadlock, they had to be made to feel that in case of extremity their power would not be found equal to their will.

HON. ATTY. GEN. CARTIER—That is because the number was unlimited.

MR. DUNKIN—If the Crown had not been able to increase the number, those honorable gentlemen might have stood out against the popular demand, until a revolution had swept them away, or they might have shrunk before the fear of it; as it was, they gave way under a milder pressure. (Hear, hear.)

HON. ATTY. GEN. CARTIER—There is a central power in all things. There is a centrifugal force and a centripetal force. Too much of either is dangerous, and what is true in the physical world, is true also in the political world.

MR. DUNKIN—Certainly. But I do not see that that has much to do with the remarks I am just now offering. (Hear, hear.) I say the elective Legislative Council was rendered necessary, in the opinion of the country, by this unfortunate state of things, even though the system then in existence was not so bad as the system now offered for our acceptance. There was then the power constitutionally given to the Crown to augment the numbers of the Legislative Council, so that the
3

gentlemen constituting that body could recede before the determined expression of the public will, as gracefully as did the House of Lords on the memorable occasion I have already alluded to. Had that House not yielded in those days of the Reform Bill, even the Crown of Great Britain might not have escaped the consequences of a bloody revolution. That House might have been constitutionally omnipotent, but its physical was not equal to its constitutional capacity. What is it that is proposed to be given to us here? A body not at all weighty in the influence of its members, and which, it is said, will have to shrink from the exercise of its prerogatives. I do not know whether it will or not. But I had rather not give to a body of men limited in number—though even so little weighty in the community—an absolute veto on all legislation, for so long as the Almighty may be pleased to continue them in life. I think a much better system could be devised—nay, I am sure of it. At all events, here is this proposed body, which, we are told, is to be Federal, but which is not to be so. We are told it is to be a constitutional check, but it is not to be that either. It is rather, I take it, a cleverly devised piece of dead-lock machinery, and the best excuse made for it is, that it will not be strong enough to do near all the harm it seems meant to do. Her Majesty's Government condemns it. It may not be necessary that we should say with very marked emphasis how we join in that condemnation. (Hear, hear.) I have then shewn, I think, Mr. SPEAKER, as regards our House of Commons, that we have not reached perfection; and that, as regards our House of Lords, we have not come near it. I pass on to the Executive. Here, too, there is to be a very wide difference between our proposed system and that of the United States. To begin, they have an elective president, chosen for a short term; with all the evils, therefore, of frequent presidential elections, aggravated by the president's allowed capacity for reëlection. No doubt, we avoid these; our Viceroy, or Governor General, is not to be elective. Nobody proposes that—I do not think anybody ever did propose it. And the authors of this project have, therefore, no great right to take credit for this, any more than for their unasked offer to continue Her Most Gracious Majesty upon the throne, or in other words, create her Queen of British North America, by the grace of the Quebec Conference! (Laughter.) This, however, Mr. SPEAKER, by the way. What is more important to notice in this connexion, is the marked distinction on which I have already touched, between the United States system, which devolves in part upon the Senate—and our system, which devolves not at all upon the Legislative Council, but wholly on the Executive Council, the duty of advising and aiding the head of the Government in the discharge of his executive functions. As I have said, in the United States the Senate has large executive functions.

Hon. Atty. Gen. CARTIER—Without responsibility for their advice. We have responsibility, and in that respect our system is better.

Mr. DUNKIN—My honorable friend says "without responsibility." I rather think not. Take the case of a senator from Massachusetts or New York. I rather think he will feel himself very distinctly responsible to the state he represents. He is not responsible to the whole people of the United States, nor is the Senate, as a whole, collectively responsible. But each senator is particularly and personally responsible to his own state, and acts under a sense of that responsibility. (Hear, hear.) Take the case which occurred a number of years ago, when President JACKSON named, as Minister to the British Court, MARTIN VAN BUREN, afterwards his successor in the presidential chair. A majority of the Senate disallowed that nomination. Did not the senators who voted for or against that nomination, do so under a weighty, practical responsibility? Every man of them did. They voted in the view and under the sanction of that responsibility; and some of them had to pay for the exercise of it. And so they do, all along. (Hear, hear.) This, however, is a digression into which I have been led by the remark of my honorable friend. I return to the line of argument I was pursuing. What I am just now shewing is, that in respect of the constitution of the executive power, this scheme urged upon our acceptance differs *toto cœlo* from the system in operation in the United States. I shall consider presently the question of its advantages or disadvantages. In the United States, as is admitted, the Senate does a certain part of what we undertake here to do by means of a Cabinet. The Federal check so exercised by the Senate renders unnecessary, for any Federal purpose, the existence of a Cabinet. Indeed they do not want a Cabinet for any purpose at all. It is not of their system. But here, with our chief magistrate not elected, we must have one. And

yet, how are we to make it work, engrafted on a system which, in its essentials, is after all more American than British? This is what I have now come to. I have to ask honorable gentlemen opposite how they are going to organize their Cabinet, for these provinces, according to this so-called Federal scheme? (Hear, hear.) I think I may defy them to shew that the Cabinet can be formed on any other principle than that of a representation of the several provinces in that Cabinet. It is admitted that the provinces are not really represented to any Federal intent in the Legislative Council. The Cabinet here must discharge all that kind of function, which in the United States is performed, in the Federal sense, by the Senate. And precisely as in the United States, wherever a Federal check is needed, the Senate has to do Federal duty as an integral part of the Executive Government. So here, when that check cannot be so got, we must seek such substitute for it as we may, in a Federal composition of the Executive Council; that is to say, by making it distinctly representative of the provinces. Well, I must say that this sort of thing is utterly variant from, and inconsistent with British practice and British principle; with the constitutional system which makes the whole Cabinet responsible for every act of government. The British Cabinet is no Cabinet of sections, but a unit. In illustration of the view which I am anxious to impress upon the judgment of the House, let me revert for a moment to our Canadian history. I can only look forward to the future by the lights given me by the past. The union of the Canadas, consummated in 1841, was a legislative union. There was nothing in it savoring ever so faintly of Federalism, unless it were the clause which declared, and quite unnecessarily declared, that there should be an equal representation in the Legislative Assembly of Upper and Lower Canada respectively. If the Union Act had merely distributed the constituencies in such a way as to give equality of representation to Upper and Lower Canada, it would have done for practical purposes all it did. But besides doing this, it quite uselessly added in terms that the numbers were to be equal—subject always, however, by a strange anomaly, to our declared power thereafter by legislation of our own to disturb that equality, if we pleased. Well, sir, when an Executive Government had to be first organized for Canada, Lord SYDENHAM was obliged to call into his Cabinet certain officials whom he found in Upper and

Lower Canada respectively, and he did so without observing any rule of equality as to their numbers. Indeed, until 1848, equality in the representation of the two sections of the province in the Cabinet was never seriously aimed at. In 1848, from considerations of a peculiar character—perhaps more personal than political—the usage was commenced, and it has since been persevered in, of having a Premier and a sub-Premier, and a Cabinet organized under them, respectively, in two sections—of course equal in numbers, or as nearly so as possible. And on this usage and in connection with it have developed themselves all those double majority and double ministry notions and practices which again of late have so constantly been leading us into all manner of constitutional difficulties. (Hear, hear.) It has been found again and again impossible to constitute a satisfactory ministry of two sections; because one or other of the two sections, if they came together on any basis of real political agreement, was so very likely not to be able to command a majority of its sectional representation in this House. It was, practically, a division of the House, as well as of the Government, into two sections—practically, all but a government by two ministries and with two Houses. We did not quite admit, to be sure, that there were two ministries; although, by the way, at one time—I refer to the time of the first proposed vote of want of confidence in the MACDONALD-DORION ministry—a motion was on the point of being made—notice of it was given—which positively did speak of a Lower Canadian ministry as contradistinguished from an Upper Canadian ministry. I go into this to shew that already, in Canada, the force of circumstances has been one too many for us, and has inflicted upon us a system more complex—less workable—than obtains in England. With us, as at home, the Constitution makes the whole Ministry, collectively, responsible for all the acts it performs; but it is well known that here, for all practical purposes, we have for years had our Ministry acting by two sections —each section with a chief of its own, to a large extent a policy of its own, and the responsibility of leading and governing a section of this House of its own. (Hear, hear.) We have been federalising our Constitution after a very new and anomalous fashion ever since 1848, and by that, more than by anything else, have been getting ourselves into that sort of difficulty in which we have lattedly found ourselves. (Hear, hear.) And now, Mr. SPEAKER, I just want to know

how this proposed scheme is going to work in this respect? As we have seen, it starts with a principle, as to the election of the House of Commons, which must involve the arraying on the floor of that House, not of a set of members of Parliament coming there to judge and to act each for the whole of British North America, but of a certain fixed number of Upper Canadians, a certain fixed number of Lower Canadians, a certain fixed number of Nova Scotians, of New Brunswickers, of Prince Edward Islanders, of Newfoundlanders, of Red River men, of men from Vancouver's Island, of British Columbia men, of Saskatchewan men—each to act there for his own province. (Hear, hear.) If we ever get all these territories laid out into provinces, we are to have just so many sections, numerically most unequal, upon the floor of this House, and the only abiding distinctions between members will be those represented by the territorial lines between their provinces. The Legislative Council, we have seen, will not be the check which these sections will require. The Executive Council has got to be that check, and in the Executive Council these sections will have to reproduce themselves. Apart from the provinces or vast territory to the west of us, we shall thus have our six such sections on the floor of the Commons House, with their six corresponding sections in the Executive Council, and six parliamentary majorities to be worked together, if possible, while hitherto we have found our two sections and two majorities one too many. Our constitutional difficulties, I repeat, are referable to that very practice, and so it is proposed that we should try a system three times—and more than three times—more complex still. (Hear, hear.) That cleverest of politicians who, for two or three years running, under such a system, shall have managed to carry on his Cabinet, leading six or more sections in our Commons House, six or more sections in the Legislative Council, and, forsooth, six or more local parliaments and lieutenant-governors, and all the rest of it besides—that gifted man who shall have done this for two or three years running, had better be sent home to teach Lords PALMERSTON and DERBY their political alphabet. The task will be infinitely more difficult than the task these English statesmen find it none too easy to undertake. (Hear, hear.)

HON. ATTY. GEN. CARTIER—There will be no difficulty.

MR. DUNKIN—The hon. gentleman never sees a difficulty in anything he is going to do.

HON. ATTY. GEN. CARTIER—And I have been generally pretty correct in that. I have been pretty successful. (Hear, hear.)

MR. DUNKIN—Pretty successful in some things—not so very successful in some others. The hon. gentleman has been a good deal favored by accident. But I am not quite certain that I believe in the absolute omniscience of anybody. (Hear, hear.) But now, if this Executive Council is to have in it, as I am sure it must have, in order to work at all, a representation of the different provinces, all or nearly all of them, let us look for a moment at what will have to be its number. There are two ways of calculating this—two sets of *data* on which to go. Either we must go upon what I may call the wants of the component parts, or we may start from the wants of the country as a whole. Suppose, then, we start from the wants o the different provinces. I take it that no section of the Confederation can well have less than one representative in the Cabinet. Prince Edward Island will want one; Newfoundland, one. A difficulty presents itself with regard to Lower Canada. On just the same principle upon which Lower Canada wants, for Federal ends, to have a proper representation in the Executive Council, on that same principle the minority populations in Lower Canada will each want, and reasonably want, the same thing. We have three populations in Lower Canada—the French-Canadians, the Irish Catholics, and the British Protestants. In other words, there are the Catholics, and the non-Catholics, and the English-speaking and the non-English-speaking, and these two cross-lines of division cut our people into the three divisions I have just indicated. Well, if in a government of this Federal kind the different populations of Lower Canada are to feel that justice is done them, none of them are to be there ignored. The consequences of ignoring them might not be very comfortable. Heretofore, according to general usage, the normal amount of representation for Lower Canada in the Executive Council has been six seats out of twelve. Of those, four may be said legitimately to belong to the French-Canadians, one to the Irish Catholics, and one to the British Protestant class. Everyone is satisfied that that is about the fairest thing that can be done. There have been times when these proportions have varied. There have been exceptional times when the British Protestant population has had to put up with a Solicitor-General out of the Cabinet,

and has done so with no very loud complaint. There has never been a time, I think, when there was not an Irish Catholic in the Cabinet. There have been times when the number of French-Canadians has been less than four, and there was then much complaint. Six members—four, one and one—are just about what you must give to please each section of Lower Canada. Well, sir, if there are to be six for Lower Canada, there must be six or seven for Upper Canada, and you cannot very well leave less than three each for Nova Scotia and New Brunswick, and, as I have said, one each for Newfoundland and Prince Edward Island; and thus you have an Executive Council of twenty or twenty-one members, besides all we might have to add for other provinces; and this, I rather think, is a little too many. The thing could not be done; for so large a Cabinet could never work. Suppose then, on the other hand, that we start with the idea of limiting the number of our Executive Council to meet what I may call the exigencies of the country as a whole. Eleven, twelve or thirteen—the latter, as an hon. member observes, is an unlucky number—will be as many as we can possibly allow. Of this number one, as before, will be wanted for Newfoundland and one for Prince Edward Island. If one is wanted for each of the little provinces, New Brunswick and Nova Scotia will be sorely discontented unless they get, at least, two apiece; and neither Lower Canada nor Upper Canada will be contented with the three left for each of them. And for Lower Canada, in particular, how will anyone divide this intractable figure between her French, Irish and British? Shall we give them one apiece, and ask the French-Canadian element to be content with one voice in a cabinet of a dozen?—or, give that element two, without satisfying it—so leaving out either the Irish or the British, to its intense disgust?—or, give the preponderating element the whole, to the intense disgust of both the others? It will be none too easy a task, sir, I think. to form an Executive Council with its three members for Lower Canada, and satisfy the somewhat pressing exigencies of her creeds and races.

HON. ATTY. GEN. CARTIER—Hear! hear!

MR. DUNKIN—The Hon. Attorney General East probably thinks he will be able to do it.

HON. ATTY. GEN. CARTIER—I have no doubt I can. (Laughter.)

MR. DUNKIN—Well, I will say this, that if the hon. gentleman can please all parties in Lower Canada with only three members in the Executive Council, he will prove himself the cleverest statesman in Canada.

HON. ATTY. GEN. CARTIER—Upon whose authority does the hon. gentleman say there will be only three?

MR. DUNKIN—The hon. gentleman has evidently not been listening to my line of argument, and I do not think that, to enlighten him, I am called upon to punish the House by going over it all again. (Hear, hear.) What I say is, that if the number of the Executive Council is fixed according to the wants of the country as a whole, and not to what I may call the local wants of the several provinces, there will be in all some eleven, twelve or thirteen members; and you will have a number so small in proportion to the various interests to be satisfied, that it will be extremely difficult to avoid serious trouble in the matter of its local distribution. On the other hand, if you give all the localities the number they had need have, on local grounds, the Council will be too large to work. It will be practically impossible to meet the needs of all the provinces; and yet, none can be left out in the cold, on pain of consequences. (Hear, hear.)

HON. ATTY. GEN. CARTIER—When the matter is brought to a test, the hon. gentleman will see that he has aggravated the difficulty.

MR. DUNKIN—SIDNEY SMITH once said of a leading Cabinet minister at home, that he would be willing at the shortest notice, either to undertake the duties of the Archbishop of Canterbury or to assume command of the Channel fleet. (Laughter.) We have some public men in this country who, in their own judgment, have ample capacity for assuming the responsibility and discharging the functions of those two high posts, and perhaps of a field marshal or commander-in-chief besides. (Renewed laughter.)

HON. ATTY. GEN. CARTIER—I would say, that although I do not feel equal to the task of commanding the Channel fleet or filling the office of Archbishop of Canterbury, I do feel equal to the work of forming an Executive Council that will be satisfactory to Upper and Lower Canada, as well as to the Lower Provinces. (Hear, hear, and laughter.)

MR. DUNKIN—Well, it will require, in my opinion, something more than bold assertion, and capacity for a hearty laugh, to overcome the difficulty that will some day or other be presented. (Hear, hear.) And now, sir, I come to speak of the relations to subsist between this Federal power and the different provinces, as compared with those between the United States and the different states. Again, the comparison has to be made much more with the United States system than with that of Great Britain; although, unfortunately, perhaps, there is in this part of the scheme some confusion of inconsistent features of the two systems. Great Britain has not yet, in any true sense of the term, federated herself with any of her colonies. She just retains a nominal supremacy over them.

MR. SCOBLE—It is a real supremacy.

MR. DUNKIN—No; it is only nominal as regards its exercise. It is not real in the sense of amounting to a substantial, practical exercise of power over the colonies. For these nearly five and twenty years past, I call to mind no legislative act of ours disallowed by the Home Government.

AN HON. MEMBER—Yes, there was one—Mr. HINCKS' Currency Act.

MR. DUNKIN—Well, I believe that was. But in that case we got our own way in effect directly afterwards. I am referring more particularly, of course, to what may be called the conduct of our own domestic affairs. There is no mistake but we have had given to us by Great Britain a control practically unlimited over our own affairs; she lets us do what we like, while professing to retain a perfect nominal supremacy over us. She appoints our Governor General, but when he comes here, he does what we want, not what she may want. She can, if she likes, disallow all our statutes; but for all practical purposes she never does. She may, if she chooses, alter or repeal the Charter of our liberties which she granted to us, but she never thinks of doing such a thing, and we know she will not. Well, here in this proposed Constitution—looking to the relations which are to subsist between the Federation and the provinces—in lieu of a real Federation, such as subsists between the United States and the different states, we find an attempt to adopt to a considerable extent the British system of a stated supremacy, not meant to be in fact the half of what it passes for in theory. But, however such a system may work as between Great

Britain and her colonies, it by no means follows that it admits of extension to this case. If the vaguely stated powers of our so-called Federation are to be merely nominal, they will be insufficient; if not nominal, they will be excessive. Either way, the United States idea of an attempted precise statement of the powers meant to be given and used, is the true one. What, then, is the system adopted in the United States, as regards these relations between the Federal power and the several states? There are two leading principles, and very sound principles, that pervade it. In the first place the United States, by its Constitution, guarantees to every state in the union a republican form of government; by which is meant a Constitution, in the main, analogous to that of the United States—an elective executive, an elective second branch, an elective popular branch—the whole without what we here call responsible government. This is what everybody understands as the republican system. Accordingly, just the same sort of thing in principle and in all its great outlines as the Constitution of the United States, is the Constitution of each separate state of the union. And in the second place, along with this uniformity in principle and outlines between the Constitution of the United States and those of the different states, there is established a very exact system of what I may call limited state autonomy. The state, within its certain range of subjects, does what it likes, and is as free to act as the United States; it has its own functions, and within the limits of those functions nobody controls it. The United States have their special functions also, and within the range of those functions can, in turn, control everything. The respective judiciary systems of the state and of the United States, are further so contrived as to be the most perfect check that can well be imagined to secure the smooth and steady working of this Federal national machinery. It is a complex piece of machinery, if you will; there are many delicate parts in it, one depending nicely upon another; but, upon the whole, it has worked pretty well for many years, and may go on working pretty well for many more.

HON. ATTY. GEN. CARTIER—But the judges are elected.

MR. DUNKIN—Does the hon. gentleman mean to tell this House that the principle of elective judges forms a part of the constitutional system of the United States? Why, sir, an elective judiciary is a mere excrescence of quite late growth, and has not fastened itself on the system of the United States at all. It is not even as yet adopted by nearly all the individual states, but only by some of them. It is an excrescence which the founders of the United States system never, I fancy, thought of, or in all human probability they would have expressly provided against it. (Hear, hear.) But now, sir, what is the system we are going to adopt according to these resolutions? What are the relations to be established between our general and local governments? We are told to take for granted that no clashing of interest or feeling need be feared; that the Federal union offered us in name will be a legislative union in reality. Yet, whoever dislikes the notion of a legislative union is assured it will be nothing of the sort. Now, sir, I do not believe that you can have all the advantages of these two systems combined in one. (Hear, hear.) A Legislative union is one thing; a Federal union is another. The same system cannot be both at once. You cannot devise a system that shall have all the advantages of the one and of the other; but it is quite possible that you may devise one that will combine the chief disadvantages of both, and that is, I fear, pretty much what this system does. (Hear, hear.) Let me first take one feature of the scheme, or, I might say, one absence of a feature from the scheme—the non-provision of anything like provincial constitutions. We are not told about them; they are kept back completely in the dark; it is part of the scheme that we are not to know what it means them to be. (Laughter.) It is part of the scheme, too, from all appearance, that they may not be at all alike. For anything I can see, Nova Scotia will have a right under this scheme to devise a system of responsible government, with a cabinet and two branches of the legislature. New Brunswick, if it pleases, may have only one legislative body, with or without responsible government. So may the Prince Edward Island people have anything they like; and the people of Newfoundland may do what they like, and so may we in Canada. Lower Canada may even have a constitution of one kind, and Upper Canada one of a totally different kind. There may be no two of our six or more local constitutions framed on the same model. (Hear, hear.) It seems to be meant that these constitutions shall be as varied as the people of the different provinces may see fit to make them nay, there are even left to the people of the different provinces the same large powers for amending them afterwards. To be sure there is the grand power of disallowance by the Federal Government, which we are told, in one and the same breath, is to be possessed by it, but never exercised.

HON. ATTY. GEN. CARTIER — The presumption is, it will be exercised in case of unjust or unwise legislation.

MR. DUNKIN—The hon. gentleman's presumption reminds me of one, perhaps as conclusive, but which DICKENS tells us failed to satisfy his Mr. BUMBLE. That hen-pecked beadle is said to have said, on hearing of the legal presumption that a man's wife acts under his control:—" If the law presumes anything of the sort, the law's a fool —a natural fool!" (Laughter.) If this permission of disallowance rests on a presumption that the legislation of our provinces is going to be unjust or unwise, it may be needed; but under that idea, one might have done better either not to allow, or else to restrict within narrower limits, such legislation. If the promised non-exercise of the power to disallow rests on a presumption that all will be done justly and wisely in the provincal legislatures, the legislative power is well given; but then there is no need, on the other hand, for the permission to disallow. (Hear, hear.) I repeat, this system, or no-system, aims at nothing like uniformity between the general and local constitutions, or between the local constitutions themselves; and in this respect, it is essentially at variance with the much wiser system adopted in the United States. It further allows of no real autonomy; in fact, the only trace of uniformity it can be said to have about it, consists in its disallowance of all autonomy to the provinces. (Hear, hear.) Now, let me take up those few features that undoubtedly are given to us, as characterizing our provincial system. Wide as we have seen the latitude is which the provinces may take in framing their constitutions, there are a few matters as to which the system lays down an iron rule. There is the appointment of a lieutenant-governor which is to be vested in the General Government. It is not said in so many words that he is to be a colonist, but I think it may be taken for granted that he will be. It is not very likely that we shall get any right honorable gentleman or eminent statesman, from home, to come out here for an appointment of that kind; and I take for granted, there-fore, that the General Government will always nominate Mr. Somebody or other, of local distinction, to this office of lieutenant governor. An hon. gentleman opposite. (I beg his pardon for noticing his gesture,) se ms never to have had the thought cross his mind, that perhaps if he were named to it, there might be a doubt in some quarters as to his entire fitness for it. (Hear, hear.) But seriously these lieutenant-governors thus selected, are all to hold office by a very peculiar tenure. They are not to be removable except by the Federal power; nor by it within the term of five years, except for cause, which cause must be stated in writing, and laid before both branches of the Federal Parliament. For five years, therefore, they may be said to hold office during good behaviour. They are to be paid, too, by the Federal power. They are to exercise the reprieving and pardoning power, subject to such instructions as they may receive from the General Government from time to time. And they are to have the initiation, by message, of all money bills, and the power to reserve bills for approval of the Federal Government. They are to have these leading functions of the nominated lieutenant governors under our system, but with one most marked difference— the attribute of non-removability. Beyond these few points, the resolutions leave us all at sea. Save as to these, they leave room, as we have seen, for the widest divergencies of constitution. To be sure, I gather one hint more, not from the resolutions themselves, but from the dispatch sent along with them to the Colonial Secretary, by the Governor General, and this is, that according to the view of our Canadian Government, the provincial legislatures had better be framed on the one chamber principle. I presume this will hardly be gainsayed by the honorable gentlemen who have laid the dispatch before us, and which supplies this feature that we cannot find in the resolutions themselves. Says the dispatch :—

For the purpose of local administration, it is proposed to have in each province an executive officer, to be appointed by the Governor, and removable by him for cause to be assigned, assisted by a legislative body. the constitution of which it is proposed to leave to the decision of the present local legislatures, subject to the approbation of the imperial Government and Parliament.

But, sir, whether our local legislatures are to be of one house or two, or however otherwise any of our provinces may experiment, in the way of variation, in framing their constitutions, at least there must everywhere be some attempted approach, in principle, to one or other of the two great divergent systems—the British on the one hand, with its responsible Cabinet—the American, on the other, without. That you cannot work the problem on the former of these two plans, I will show presently. For the latter, Mr. SPEAKER, in the States, it is always carried on with two elective houses, never with one, and with an elective governor; and all are chosen for terms that are not long. It could not be made to work otherwise. An appointed governor, holding independently, for a term not short, and above all, with only one House, is an experiment as new and unpromising as need be. For a moment, before going further, I revert to the principle on which the Federal Executive is to be constituted. We are promised there a cabinet, responsible after the British model, and strangely and anomalously as we have seen that it will have to be organized, in sections to represent our provinces, we must understand that the British principle of its joint responsibility is to be and will be carried out. But it is of the essence of responsible government, that with its responsibility such government should have power. No ministry can be answerable for the entire government of a country, unless it has the power to control in some way or other, and to the requisite extent, the course of affairs. If we are going to build up or suffer in the country any power too strong for it to deal with, it will cease to be responsible. It must be able to overcome opposition, and that in a constitutional manner. Yet, according to this scheme, independently of and besides all the difficulties our sectionally-organized Federal Cabinet will find in dealing with its sectionally-organized Federal Legislature, it is to have these provincial governments also, to embarrass it. Let these last be what you will, responsible or republican, or some of them the one and some the other, so soon as they begin to act for themselves, so soon you have got powers in action that cannot long move together without clashing, and yet neither of which can overcome the other, unless by practically destroying it, or in other words, by revolution. (Hear, hear.) Whether we adopt one system or another, we must create the proper machinery for carrying out whatever system we adopt. And the plain truth is,

that the Federal system is simply inconsistent with the first principles that must prevail in a properly organized British responsible central government. (Hear, hear.) Indeed, aside even from Federalism, the British system and the republican are antagonist in principle; neither of them will work mixed up with the other. You must be content with one or other, and must not commit the folly of attempting any new, untried, mongrel system, or compound of the two—such as nobody can shew to be capable of being worked at all. And now, Mr. SPEAKER, let us just follow out the course of our distinguished fellow-colonist who is trying to govern some one of our provinces, under this proposed amalgamation of the two systems. We will suppose him a most admirably fitted person for the post, the functions of which he is called upon to exercise; but he must necessarily have one or two causes of incapacitation, so to speak, for it. When Her Majesty appoints a governor to come out to Canada, or any other colony, she is presumed by every one here to have named somebody holding a good position at home, and somebody against whom no one in the colony can have any ground of dislike. He comes with a social rank and *status* presumedly higher than that of the people whom he is here to meet with and govern. Every one is disposed to recognise in him the representative of Her Majesty; and he has every chance of maintaining himself in that pleasant attitude— that of administering his government to the satisfaction, so far as such a thing is possible, of all parties. In adopting the views of his constitutional advisers, he is not called upon to give up any views which he may himself be thought to entertain. He can express to the people's representatives the views of his Cabinet, whether they be conservative or reform, or even though they be conservative this session and reform the next, without any sacrifice of position, no matter what his own political views may have been in the Mother Country. But suppose any of our politicians, whether of this province or of any other in the Confederacy, say Canada, Newfoundland or Nova Scotia, to be assuming this *rôle* of lieutenant-governor in any of our provinces. He has this disadvantage to begin with; he has to that moment been passing through that ordeal of abuse under which every prominent public man in this country must have suffered before attaining any distinction what-

25

ever. (Hear, hear.) When a politician, Mr. SPEAKER, in the United States, who is obnoxious to the ill-will of any large body of the people, is there elected to be Governor of his state, the halo of his election surrounds him with a something of political glory that throws into shade any stains on his political reputation. But if the governors of the several states of the American Union were appointed from Washington, do you think the people would put up with the results of such appointment, as they now do with those of their own choice; when they might feel that the man was even a despised, dishonest man, and his appointment as well an insult as a wrong? Who does not know that our chief public men of all parties have been so assailed, as to be held at this moment at a painfully low value by the large section of our people who have differed from their views? I do not say that they have deserved this fate, but the fact is undeniable that they have met it. Let any one of our dozen or twenty most prominent Canadian politicians be named Lieutenant-Governor of Upper or of Lower Canada, would not a large and powerful class of the community in either case to be governed, be very likely to resent the nomination as an insult? Do not tell me that we are entering upon a new era, that all such things are passed away, that we are to have a political millennium, by virtue of this Confederation? Come what may, we are going to have pretty sharp contests for place and power in the future as in the past. No matter over what colony appointed, or from what colony coming, a lieutenant-governor will have hard cards to play, and will have very much to put up with from the people over whom he is set, on this mere score of his past political exploits. And he will not find it easy, either, to get along without exciting a good deal of ill-feeling, as he goes. He has been known as a politician, and will be held to be favorable or unfavorable to this or that party in the province he governs. He will have stepped into position as a statesman of the Confederation. No man so placed will be able to blot the record of his past, or deny his participation in this, that and the other proceeding, which his opponent may choose to brand as perhaps next to criminal; how then will he be able to hold that position of equilibrium between political parties, which, if he is not to fail utterly in his *rôle* of governor, he must maintain? He will be suspected, watched, attacked, vilified; must stick by friends and

punish enemies; cannot win respect, esteem and sympathy, as a stranger might. Nor will he be free from another source of embarrassment. I incline to think there will be a sort of distinction between the two classes of politicians to grow up under our proposed Confederation. There will be those who will aim at and get seats in the Federal Legislature, and who may be denominated the senior or higher class of our politicians. It will be from this class that men will get into the Federal Executive Council, into high-caste judgeships, lieutenant-governorships, and other high places of the new system—"the chief seats in the synagogue." The lower seats, with their less tempting prizes, will be left to the junior or lower class of our politicians. But if anything ever so little like responsible government is to be carried out in the provinces, while the lieutenant-governors must be taken from the former of these two classes, the members of any cabinets or quasi-cabinets that they may have (not to say their provincial Premiers even, very likely), must be taken from the latter class. Do you mean to tell me that a governor chosen from among our politicians, of what I may call high caste, will put up with much of control from a lot of politicians of low caste, sitting at his sham council board or forming his sham legislature? I fancy he will want to have—and will be held by his people to be wanting to have—a vast deal more of power than they will like, or than any system ever so little free can allow of. And meantime, what of the power behind, and nominally above him —the Federal Executive—with its Premier, sections, and what not? Once named, he is likely to feel every inch a governor; might perhaps run round to the Premier and Ministry that had named him, and tell them in effect, though probably not in so many words: "I am here and you are there. I shall be careful not to give you sufficient cause for so bold a step as my dismissal, but there is a good deal I can do. I am here for five years; and your tenure of office is less certain." He may be drawn into this attitude by differences growing up between himself and them. Or, the Federal Cabinet may so change its composition or policy as to force such attitude upon him. Why, Mr. SPEAKER, you may have a Lieutenant-Governor—say of Lower Canada—in open quarrel with the Premier who named him, or with a successor of such Premier; the two, may be, not speaking in the streets! He has

4

his seat for five years, and the unfortunate Federal Premier, his supposed master, whose views do not agree with his, may—

A MEMBER—Whistle! (Laughter)

Mr DUNKIN—Yes, may whistle—may find his Lieutenant-Governor counter-working him in Parliament, in the Provincial Legislature, everywhere; and perhaps, in the encounter, may catch a very ugly fall. (Laughter.) Mr. SPEAKER, let me once again make reference to Canadian history. Just before the union of the Canadas, and after it, the late Lord SYDENHAM, who was certainly not a fool, thought he would try a political experiment. I believe he made no secret of its being, to his own mind, an experiment, nor yet of the fact that he did not suppose it would so far succeed as to last long. He was very anxious to introduce into Canada a municipal system. Well, he tried first to get such a system embodied in the Union Act; but he failed in that. He afterwards got his enactment passed as he wished, for Lower Canada, by the Special Council, and for Upper Canada by the Canadian Parliament at its first session. That system had in it certain features of this scheme now proposed for our Confederation. Each municipal district was to have its warden appointed by the Governor General, and to have its elected district council, or little legislature of one chamber. The powers of that little legislature, or large municipal body, were well stated. There was no mistake as to just how far it could go. The power of disallowing by-laws passed by it, and also that of nominating, the warden, were carefully reserved to Government. And, mind you, my Lord SYDENHAM did not make the blunder of letting his wardens hold otherwise than during pleasure. He kept in his own hands all needed control over them; and, by the way, he kept, too, what was most material, the power of dissolving any refractory council, in the hands of Government. The whole thing was nicely arranged, and was meant to work, and Lord SYDENHAM probably thought it would work for some few years, and that then the districts would outgrow the system, and elect their own wardens and pass their by-laws freely. But, Mr. SPEAKER, the plan never did work at all, neither in Lower nor in Upper Canada; and the first thing done by the next Parliament was to sweep it all away—nominated wardens and power of disallowing by-laws together. Everybody saw and felt that it was a real power and not a sham, that was so reserved to Government. And so it will be in this case. Your Lieutenant-Governor will be felt to have a real power, not a sham one. What your petty districts would not put up with five and twenty years ago, your provinces will not put up with now. Is a larger illustration wanted? One comes readily to hand. The Imperial Government used once to try the experiment of sending out governors to colonies having representative institutions, without instructing them to pay due deference to those institutions, and it led to a most lamentable failure. (Hear, hear.) Are we going to try to work, in all these provinces, a worse system than that which, when worked from the Colonial Office at home, resulted in what Lord DURHAM well called "constituted anarchy?" If we are, how long may we count on putting off the conflict of authority that shall end in a complete crash of the entire fabric? (Hear, hear.) But, Mr. SPEAKER, I have not come to the crowning difficulties of this case, even yet. Not at all. Between the states of the United States, as I have already stated, while there is an essential identity of constitution, there is at the same time a carefully distinct separation of powers and functions. I do not say that the dividing line is drawn exactly where it should be, but that there is a distinct dividing line, no one can gainsay. But how do we stand here, Mr. SPEAKER, as to the attributes of our own provincial legislatures and governments, on the one hand, and those of the Federal power on the other? Do we follow American example, and give so much to the union and the rest to the provinces; or so much to them, and the rest to it? Either rule would be plain; but this plan follows neither. It simply gives us a sort of special list for each; making much common to both, and as to much more, not shewing what belongs to either. I cannot go now—it is impossible for me at this hour of the night to go—into detail on this head. I can give no more than some few specimens; and I take first the three subjects of the fisheries, agriculture, and immigration. These three subjects are equally assigned to the General Legislature on the one hand, and the Provincial Legislature on the other. It is provided by the 45th resolution, that in all such cases, wherever any statutes of the general and local parliaments clash, those of the General Parliament shall override those of the local. So that in these matters of the fisheries, agriculture and immigration, either the local legislatures must not legislate at all, or if they do the General Legislature may at any time undo anything they may have done. One can easily foresee any amount of clashing of authority in such cases. Fishery regulations of all sorts — bounties perhaps; the thousand questions affecting agriculture. Or to take just one that suggests itself as to immigration; one province wishes, perhaps, to encourage immigration of a certain kind, say, for instance, from the continent of Europe. It is a legitimate wish; but the Federal Legislature may, perhaps, in the varying shifts of public opinion, adopt a different policy, and reverse all that the province may have done. To what end give powers to the local parliaments which may thus be taken away at any moment by the Federal Legislature? (Hear, hear.) But, Mr. SPEAKER, there are a hundred other cases as to which I could satisfy the House, had I time for doing so, that more or less of this confusion arises. Take the subject of marriage and divorce for one—a subject on which there is a great deal of local prejudice and feeling, and into which even religious convictions largely enter. That matter is given to the General Legislature. But on the other hand the larger matter, civil rights — of which this of marriage and divorce, from one point of view, forms a mere part—is given to the local legislatures. I turn to another matter, haphazard—the subjects of railway legislation, of railway incorporation, and of railway amalgamation. What Legislature has power in these matters under this scheme? I am not sure that there are not here as nice a lot of pretty little questions as one would desire to see in a summer's day. And I am not alone in the matter of this criticism. Her Majesty's Colonial Secretary expresses an opinion, rather diplomatically, it is true, but still an opinion on this point; and what does the Colonial Secretary say?—

The point of principal importance to the practical well-working of the scheme, is the accurate determination of the limits between the authority of the central and that of the local legislatures in their relation to each other. It has not been possible to exclude from the resolutions, some provisions which appear to be less consistent than might, perhaps, have been desired with the simplicity of the system. But, upon the whole, it appears to Her Majesty's Government that precautions have been taken which are obviously intended—["intended;" he does not say "calculated"]—which are obviously intended to secure to the Central Government the means of effective action throughout the several provinces, and to guard against those evils which must inevitably arise if any doubt were permitted to exist as to the respective limits of central and local authority.

It is perfectly plain from this that Her Majesty's Government could see that whatever may have been the intention, there has been a good deal of short-coming between it and the execution. (Hear, hear.) A thing is not done by being merely intended. I will take now a criticism on the same point from the London *Times*. In an article most eulogistic of these resolutions on the whole, the writer in the London *Times* says—"But the most important clause in the whole resolutions, and unfortunately by no means the easiest to understand, is the one which defines the powers of the Central Federal Legislature." He then quotes the words of the resolutions, and goes on to say :—

It is exceedingly difficult to construe these provisions. First, general powers of legislation are given in the widest terms to the General Parliament; then a power is given especially to make laws on thirty-seven subjects, one of those being all matters of a general character not exclusively reserved to the local legislatures. Nothing is exclusively reserved to the local legislatures, and it would seem, therefore, that the effect of this clause is to cut the power of central legislation down to matters of a general character—a most vague and unsatisfactory definition, and one sure, if it be retained, to produce conflict and confusion. In the same way, what are matters of a private and local nature not assigned to the General Parliament? We have failed to discover any matters of a private and local nature which are so assigned, and therefore the power will be limited by the words "private" and "local," so that the effect of these clauses will be that, beyond the subjects attributed to each, the Central Legislature will have jurisdiction over general matters, whatever they are, and the Local Legislature over local matters, whatever they are ; while it is in the highest degree doubtful what the courts would consider general and what local, and whether the Central Legislature has any concurrent jurisdiction over private and local matters or no.

The writer in the *Times* goes on to say—and I have great respect for the opinions of these writers when they criticise what they understand, though I have none whatever for them when they take it upon themselves to tell us what we know a good deal better than they :—

These inaccuracies are probably the result of a succession of compromises, and we can do no better service to the federative movement than by thus early pointing them out. The resolutions ask for the co-operation of the Local and Imperial Parliaments for the purpose of giving them effect, and we have no doubt that before they assume the form of law they will have under gone consideration and scrutiny fully commensurate to their importance.

I rather think this writer had little idea of what we were to be asked to do! He little thought that there was not a word of alteration to be allowed; that these resolutions were to be laid before Parliament, and that Parliament would be required to swallow them at once, defects and all. (Hear, hear.) Well, Mr. SPEAKER, I have stated what. in diplomatic phrase, are the views of Her Majesty's Government, and I have also read those of the leading journal; and now I desire to quote a few expressions from the last number of the *Edinburgh Review.* The *Edinburgh Review* is about as good an authority as can be cited on a question of this kind, for its articles are never lightly written.

HON. J. S. MACDONALD—It is the organ of the Liberal-Whig party in Great Britain.

MR. DUNKIN—Certainly, it is a most important and influential publication; and there are a few words that I desire to quote from an article it contains on this subject. The article is in the last or January number of the *Review,* and purports to be in commendation of this scheme. After giving the words of the resolutions themselves on the subject, and especially their residuary legacy, if I may so call it, to the General Legislature, of all matters of a general character not specially and exclusively reserved for the local parliaments, this probably not undistinguished writer remarks—"Obviously very loosely expressed; for what are matters of a general character, and who is to decide whether a matter is of a general character or not? * * We should prefer to the foregoing enumeration of the powers of the Federal Parliament, a simple declaration that all powers are given to it except those expressly reserved to the several members of the Confederation." And in another part of the same article, reverting to the same subject, we have these words—" And although the distinction attempted to be drawn between general and local matters is in some re-pects scarcely traceable in the draft minutes of the Conference "—Yes, sir, so this writer calls them, their looseness of expression evidently leading him to take them for something far short of the solemnly drawn treaty they are now set up for,—though this distinction, says he, is hardly traceable in these draft minutes, *"the object they had in view* is sufficiently clear and intelligible." Perhaps so; or perhaps that object was little more than to give people to understand that somehow or other the General Government and

Parliament were to have great power, and the provincial governments and parliaments none too much. Any way, the idea is very like that of the Colonial Secretary's despatch, and the two run rather to the tune of the left-handed compliment paid SLENDER, " I think my cousin *meant well.*"

HON. J. S. MACDONALD—Quote the concluding part of the article.

MR. DUNKIN—I shall do so before I sit down, if my strength allows me to complete my argument. I pass now to another matter, as to which further capacities for conflict are very well laid out for us. In the framing of the United States Constitution they did not forget to provide for a district of Columbia, for a territory within which the power of Congress and the General Government was to be perfectly and unmistakably supreme for all purposes. And they did not forget to declare that the powers, legislative and otherwise, of the Federal authority, were to be complete over all the vast territories belonging to the nation, and over all its smaller properties, such as forts, arsenals, dockyards and the like. We have nothing of the kind here; and, at least as regards the seat of Government, this is not a mere forget. We find it stated that " The seat of Government of the Federated Provinces shall be Ottawa, subject to the royal prerogative." It is distinctly laid down as a part of our system that the royal prerogative; the right to change the seat of the Federal Government at will, is to be maintained. But I venture to say that the maintaining of that right is simply inconsistent with the practical working out of a Federal system. And this is a matter involving a good deal of anomaly, as honorable gentlemen will see when they begin to think of it. The Governor General or Viceroy, the all but king of this Confederacy, with his all but Imperial Government, and all but Imperial Legislature, constituted no matter how, resident within the territorial jurisdiction of a subordinate province! The police of the Federal capital, not Federal but provincial! That thing won't do. The framers of the Constitution of the United States knew it would not do, and therefore they were particular to give power to their General Government to acquire and hold and control and legislate for, in all respects, as they liked, a territory within which they could reign and rule and have no subordinate authority over them. We have not got to Ottawa yet, but suppose the seat of Government were in Ottawa—perhaps we may yet get it there—it might so happen that some Honorable Premier of the Federal Administration may not be on speaking terms with the Lieutenant-Governor of Upper Canada; or at least, there may be between them the most decided, thorough, unmistakably proclaimed antagonism of views and feeling. It is easy to imagine that a Premier in that position, and a Lieutenant Governor in that position, could between them make a Viceroy very uncomfortable; and that the result might be the bringing up of a great many ticklish questions for adjudication by the various authorities. It is clear there is a defect here, which might lead to plenty of trouble. But it is said—"Oh! there won't be any trouble; men are in the main sensible, and won't try to make trouble." Well, sir, if this is so, if there is this general disposition to be sensible, and make things work well, I just want to know how we come to have had four crises in two years? (Hear, hear.) There is another matter, intimately connected with this, to which also I must pass on. I said a little while ago, that the United States system was one of exceeding skill as regards the constitution of the judiciary. DE TOCQUEVILLE, and every other writer who has treated of the United States, has awarded it this praise; and they are right. Each state has its own judiciary; and the United States have theirs; and the functions of the two are most carefully laid down, so that no serious trouble has ever arisen from their clashing. The judiciary of the United States is undoubtedly the most conservative and strongest bulwark of their whole system. (Hear, hear.) What then are we going to do on this head? Just as we have forgotten all about difficulties where the seat of government is concerned, so here. We are not quite sure whether we are going to have any distinctively federal judiciary or not. There is a power given to have one—there may be one; but we are expressly told that perhaps there will not be. But what are we told on the other hand? Oh, there is no doubt whatever, according to the resolutions laid before us — no doubt whatever—that whether we have a Federal judiciary or not, the provincial judiciaries are to be a sort of joint institutions. And a very curious kind of co-partnership the Federal Government and the provincial governments —the Federal Legislature and the provincial legislatures—are thus to have in the judicial institutions of the country, generally. All the courts, judges, and other judicial officers of the provinces are to be, for all manner of federal purposes, servants of the Federal Government. There is an old saying, "No man can serve two masters." But all these unfortunate courts, and all their officers, and specially all their judges, must serve two masters, whether they can or not. All the Superior Court judges—and, in Upper Canada, the judges of the County Courts—are to be named and paid by the Federal authority, and are only to be removable by the Federal authority, on a joint address of the two Houses of the Federal Parliament. But, on the other hand, the provinces are to constitute the courts—(hear, hear)—are to say what their functions shall be—what the number of the judges—how they are to perform their functions—are to give them more work or less— to make their work pleasant or disagreeable, high work or dirty work, as they like. (Hear, hear.) In this way they can wrong a judge just as much as they please; the only check on them being the power of the Federal Government to disallow their legislation. The Federal Government, forsooth, names the judges, and pays them, and alone can remove them. Does that take away the power from the local parliaments and governments, the power to change the constitution of the court, to change it in the way most distasteful to those judges, to legislate away the court altogether, to legislate down its functions in such a manner as may drive the judge to resign? And we are told there will be no clashing! (Hear.) I have no doubt the Hon. Attorney General East thinks he could manage courts on this system; could have one authority constituting the courts and another naming and removing the judges, and have the system work harmoniously. He may think so. I do not. I am satisfied if ever the scheme is tried, it will be found that it will not work. Human nature is human nature; and here is a first-rate lot of matters to quarrel over, and to quarrel over seriously. Why, there is even a special refinement of confusion as to criminal matters. Criminal procedure is to be federal; civil procedure, provincial; criminal legislation, proper, is to be federal; but with a most uncertain quantity of what one may call legislation about penalties, provincial; civil rights, in the main, provincial; but with no one can tell how much of federal interference and over-ruling, and all with courts provincial in constitution, but whose judges hold by federal tenure and under federal pay. I pity the poor man who is at once a criminal judge and a civil judge. Between the clashing of his masters and the clashing of his book authorities, he had better mind what he is about, with the painful doubt rising at every turn whether provincial legislation may not be overridden by federal legislation. His province may well have legislated on what it holds a local matter, while the Federal Parliament may have legislated on it, thinking it a federal matter. Anywhere there may well be some bit of federal legislation contradicting something in a local statute. And do our resolutions say that the federal statute shall always override the local statute ? No, only in cases where there is concurrent jurisdiction. And yet our judge who is to decide these nice questions is paid by one power and removable by that power, and may have his functions taken away and be persecuted to the death by the other. He will have a bad time of it. Well, Mr. SPEAKER, I have so far been dealing with matters, nearly all of which may be said to be general to every part of this great Confederacy ; but now I must ask the attention of the House for a few moments, to some sources of misunderstanding which may more particularly make trouble, unless human nature ceases to be human nature within this Canada of ours. There are in Canada, and especially in Lower Canada, the two differences of language and faith ; and there is no doubt that the real reasons which have rendered, or are supposed to have rendered necessary this plan of a sort of Federal Government, are referable to this fact. This machinery is devised, on purpose to meet a possible or probable clashing of races and creeds in Canada, and particularly in Lower Canada. Now, in the United States, when their constitutional system was adopted, the framers of it must have foreseen, of course, that controversy would arise on the subjects of state rights and slavery. There was a jealousy between the small states and the large, and the commencement of a dissent between the Northern and the Southern States of the republic. There was undoubtedly a foreshadowing of trouble on the subject of slavery, though, by the way, slavery was to all appearance dying out rapidly in the Northern States, not so rapidly in the Southern. How, then, did the framers of that Constitution undertake to deal with these foreseen troubles, these questions of state rights and slavery ? Sir, they did all they possibly could to keep both out of sight—to bury them—that they might not rise up in the future to give trouble. It is true that in so doing they but buried the dragon's teeth, and that these, all buried as they were, have yet since sprung up, armed

men ; but so far as they could, they kept them down, kept them from growing, prevented recognition of them at that time and for long after. Well, how are we going to carry out this scheme of ours ? Are we burying, or are we of set choice sowing, our dragon's teeth ? Are we trying to keep our difficulties out of the way, to bury them out of sight, that we may smooth our way for the future lessening of them ? I think not. On the contrary, we are setting ourselves as deliberately as we well can to keep up the distinctions and the differences which exist among us, to hold them constantly in everybody's sight—in the hope, I suppose, that while everybody is looking at them intently, somehow or other no one may see them at all. (Laughter.) In the United States, be it remembered, they started with their states sovereign and independent. From that they went into their system of confederation, which was a great improvement; and from that they went on into their present federal-national constitution. At each step they were moving to limit state rights, and also, indirectly, the extent and influence of slavery. It is true they did not altogether succeed in this policy, but their want of success has been mainly owing to circumstances over which they could exercise no control. We in Canada, for the last twenty-five years, have been legislatively united, and we have worked that union in a federal spirit. We complain that, as a result of this, the distinctions which exist among us have become so prominent—the truth being, that it is rather this proposed change which is suddenly bringing them into startling prominence— we have worked that union, however, I say, in a federal spirit, and it is said to have produced or aggravated a certain state of feud amongst us ; and now, for the purpose of perpetuating this state of feud, we are going to effect a professedly Federal union which is even expressly recommended to us, or to many of us, as meant and calculated to be so worked as to amount, for all practical purposes, to disunion. Under it Lower Canada has all sorts of special exceptions made, as the phrase runs, in her favor. The Legislative Council is to be named in a peculiar manner, so far as its members from Lower Canada are concerned. The other provinces may have their laws made uniform, but an exception in this respect is made for Lower Canada, and as if to make it apparent that Lower Canada is never to be like the rest of the Confederation, it is carefully provided that the General Parliament may make uniform the laws of the other provinces only—that is to say, provided those provinces consent to it, but by inference it cannot extend this uniformity to Lower Canada, not even if she should wish it. Supposing, even, that the other provinces were to desire to adopt our Lower Canadian system, according to the letter of this Constitution, one would say they cannot do it. They may become uniform among themselves, but Lower Canada, even though her people were to wish it, must not be uniform with them. Again, as to education, exceptions of some sort are to be made in Lower Canada, and indeed in Upper Canada too, though no one can tell to what extent these exceptions are or are not to be carried. Thus, in one way and another, Lower Canada is to be placed on a separate and distinct footing from the other provinces, so that her interests and institutions may not be meddled with. I say this system, as a whole, and these peculiarities and exceptions in regard to Lower Canada, are adopted with a special view to remedy our Canadian difficulties of race and creed. But, sir, this is no way at all of avoiding or lessening trouble from this cause. It is idle to pretend that by this system collision is going to be prevented. Under the legislative union of the Canadas, even worked as it has been, the tendency of the minorities in Upper and Lower Canada, respectively, has been towards the maintenance of the union—towards the avoidance of all intemperate language and prejudiced feelings—towards the pulling down of the feuds that before divided them and the respective majorities. And the result has been, that while just before the union the feud between the races in Lower Canada was at its highest and bitterest point, it has since then all but disappeared. The complaint of Upper Canadian politicians has been that they could not set the British and French races in Lower Canada by the ears, that they could not get the former, either as British or as Protestants, to join with them in a crusade against the Lower Canadian majority.

Mr. A. MACKENZIE—Who made that complaint?

Mr. DUNKIN—I do not say that it has been said in words, but it has been in spirit.

Mr. A. MACKENZIE—No, no. (Hear, hear.)

Mr. DUNKIN—Yes; the complaint has been made, perhaps not in that particular form, but certainly in that spirit. The British of Lower Canada have been again and again told they were worse than their French neighbors, for not casting in their lot with the people of Upper Canada. (Hear, hear.) Well, Mr. SPEAKER, undoubtedly, before the union, Lower Canada, as I have said, was the place where the war of races was at its height; and that war of races did not nearly cease for a number of years after. But the strife did very gradually lessen, and a better and more friendly feeling has for some time prevailed, in both camps. Indeed, there has been a more tolerant state of feeling in both camps, than in any other community so divided as to race and creed, that I know of. But the moment you tell Lower Canada that the large-sounding powers of your General Government are going to be handed over to a British-American majority, decidedly not of the race and faith of her majority, that moment you wake up he old jealousies and hostility in their strongest form. By the very provisions you talk of for the protection of the non-French and non-Catholic interests, you unfortunately countenance the idea that the French are going to be more unfair than I believe they wish to be. For that matter, what else can they well be? They will find themselves a minority in the General Legislature, and their power in the General Government will depend upon their power within their own province and over their provincial delegations in the Federal Parliament. They will thus be compelled to be practically aggressive, to secure and retain that power. They may not, perhaps, wish to be; they may not, perhaps, be aggressive in the worst sense of the term.—I do not say that they certainly will be; but whether they are or not, there will certainly be in this system the very strongest tendencies to make them practically aggressive upon the rights of the minority in language and faith, and at the same time to make the minority most suspicious and resentful of aggression. The same sort of alienation, as between the two faiths, will be going on in Upper Canada. Note of warning is already given by this scheme, to both parties, that they prepare for fight; and the indications, I regret to say, are that such note of warning is not to be given in vain. (Hear, hear.) The prejudices of the two camps are once more stirred to their depths; and if this scheme goes into operation, they will separate more and more widely, and finally break out into open war, unless, indeed, it shall work very differently from what any one can now imagine. If provincial independence is to be crushed down by a General Government careless of local majorities, then you will have this war. Or, if on the other hand, the policy of the Federal Executive should be to give effect to the aggregate will of the several local majorities, at whatever sacrifice of principle, still then you will have this war. The local minorities—threatened with elimination, in their alarm and jealousy, will be simply desperate, ready for any outbreak of discontent at any moment. Take a practical case. Suppose the rule adopted, of not having an Executive Council inconveniently large, Lower Canada, as we have seen, can then only have three members of it; and if all these three are French-Canadians—as they almost must be, because the French cannot put up with less than three out of twelve—how will not the Irish Catholics and the British Protestants feel themselves aggrieved? You cannot help it. They must in that case feel deeply aggrieved, and so feeling, they will cause troubles. The Irish Catholics will be told, I suppose, " Oh, you will have an Irish Catholic member of the Government to look to from Newfoundland;" and if so, they will have to guide themselves by some sort of Irish-Catholic Newfoundland rule of policy, and not by any rule ever so little savoring of a regard for larger or higher principle. The British Protestants, in their turn, will be told: "You have a majority of your own tongue and faith from Upper Canada and the Lower Provinces; you must be content with that, and look to their members of the Government for such care as you may need in the matter of your affairs." " Oh, we must, must we ?" will be the answer; " then we will square our conduct, not by any rule for British America or even Lower Canada, but by the shifting exigencies of prejudice or passion, whatever they may be, in Upper Canada and your Lower Provinces." (Hear, hear.) These discontented elements in Lower Canada, depend upon it, will create no small confusion ; and among those thus driven into making trouble, there will be not a few whose preferences will even be American, and who will appeal to outside influences for protection. Such will be the legitimate effect of this system; and if any one tells me that it will be conducive to the peace and good government of this country, I say he prophecies in a way that I cannot understand. Thank God, Mr. SPEAKER, I do not need, as I stand here, to defend myself from any charge of bigotry as against any sect or party. There was a time in Canada when it was most difficult for any person who spoke my tongue to stand up and say that the French-Canadians ought not to be politically exterminated from the face of the earth. I stood out steadfastly against that doctrine then. I remember well the painful events of that sad time. I foresee but too distinctly the fearful probability there is of that time coming again, through the adoption of these resolutions. And I do not shrink from the danger of being misunderstood or misrepresented, when I now stand up here and warn the country of this danger. If trouble of this sort ever arises, it is one that will extend very rapidly over the whole Confederacy. In all parts of it, in every province, there are minorities that will be acted upon by that kind of thing. In the Lower Provinces, and in Newfoundland, things are but too ripe for the outburst of hostilities of this description. Talk, indeed, in such a state of things, of your founding here by this means " a new nationality "—of your creating such a thing—of your whole people here rallying round its new Government at Ottawa. Mr. SPEAKER, is such a thing possible ? We have a large class whose national feelings turn towards London, whose very heart is there; another large class whose sympathies centre here at Quebec, or in a sentimental way may have some reference to Paris; another large class whose memories are of the Emerald Isle; and yet another whose comparisons are rather with Washington ; but have we any class of people who are attached, or whose feelings are going to be directed with any earnestness, to the city of Ottawa, the centre of the new nationality that is to be created? In the times to come, when men shall begin to feel strongly on those questions that appeal to national preferences, prejudices and passions, all talk of your new nationality will sound but strangely. Some other older nationality will then be found to hold the first place in most people's hearts. (Hear, hear.) Mr. SPEAKER, it is only right that I should state to the House that I have not reached within a long distance of the point which I had hoped to reach before sitting down ; but

I feel compelled to ask the indulgence of the House, from my strength being insufficient to bear me through. (Cheers.) The debate was then adjourned, Mr. DUNKIN having the floor again for next day.

——o——

MR. DUNKIN, continuing his speech from yesterday, said—Mr. SPEAKER, when the kindness of the House permitted me to resume my seat last evening, I was comparing the constitutional system of the proposed Confederacy with the Constitution of the United States primarily, and with that of Great Britain secondarily. I had gone over several leading points of comparison ; and it will be in the recollection of the House, no doubt, that I had compared the composition of our proposed House of Commons with that of the House of Representatives of the United States ; and I endeavored to shew, and I think I had shewn, that we were departing altogether from the principles upon which the British House of Commons is constituted, and taking up *mal à propos*, an l unfortunately, the least inviting features of the composition of the American House of Representatives. It is proposed to adopt here a plan which has a direct tendency to place on the floor of our House of Commons a number of provincial delegations, and not a number of independent members of parliament. The tendency is therefore towards a system antagonistic to, and inconsistent with, those principles on which the British Constitution reposes. With provincial delegations, rather than members of parliament, on the floor of the Federal Legislature, we are not likely to have that political longevity, whether of men or parties, without which the British system of government can hardly exist. Turning then to the Legislative Council, and comparing its constitution with that of the Senate of the United States—the principles governing the former are diametrically opposite to those on which the latter is founded. The Senate of the United States forms an excellent federal check upon the House of Representatives, partly owing to the way in which it is constituted, and partly on account of the powers given to it, and which are not proposed to be given to our Legislative Council. All that can be said of it is, that it is proposed to be constituted upon almost the worst principles that could have been adopted. It seems as if it were so constituted for the mere purpose of leading to a dead-lock. The members of it are not to represent our provinces at all, but are to be named by the Federal power itself, for life, and in numbers to constitute a pretty numerous body, but without any of the peculiar functions wisely assigned to the Senate of the United States. In fact, the federal battle that must be fought will have to be fought in the House of Commons and in the Executive Council, very much more than in the Legislative Council. Turning then to the Executive Council, I had shown that it is a necessary consequence of the proposed system, that we are to have not merely a House of Commons cut up into sections, but also an Executive Council cut up in the same unfortunate way. You can get nothing else in the nature of a real federal check. Your federal problem will have to be worked out around the table of the Executive Council. But this principle, which must enter into the formation of the Executive Council, is clearly inconsistent with the principle of the British Constitution, which holds the whole Cabinet jointly responsible for every act of the Government. In our present union of the Canadas, we have latterly gone upon the plan of having almost two ministries. The plan urged upon our acceptance purposes the experiment of six or more sections in the Executive Council, instead of the two that we have found one too many. Among the difficulties that will grow out of that plan is this, the absolute necessity of either having an Executive Council that will be ridiculously too numerous, or else one that will represent the different provinces in sections entirely too small. From this comparison of these three leading features, I had passed on to consider the relations of the Federal Government with the several provinces, comparing them 'with the relations subsisting between the United States Government and the governments of the several states of the American Union. The several states of the neighboring republic commenced their existence as states with all their constitutions constructed on the same general plan as that of the United States, and in fact the same republican principles underlie all their governmental institutions, municipal, state and federal. But it is here proposed, that while we are to start with a system of general government, part British, part republican, part neither, it is to be an open question, left to the decision of each separate province, what kind of local constitution is

5

to be constructed for itself. Each province must, of course, have an elective chamber, but as to a second chamber, that is to be as each local legislature may see fit. Some, probably, will have it elective, while others may dispen e with it entirely. Then, looking to the appointment of the lieutenant-governors, and the tenure by which they are to hold office, it becomes about as clear as day that you cannot carry on responsible government in the provinces, but must have in them all a system that is neither British nor republican, and that, I believe, will be found to be totally unworkable. Turning to the assignment of powers to the Federal Government on the one hand, and the local or provincial governments on the other, we meet again with the unhappy contrast between the wisdom displayed on that point in the Constitution of the United States, and the lack of wisdom in the arrangement proposed for adoption here. There is, in the United States' system, a clear and distinct line drawn between the functions of the general and state governments. Some may not like the idea of state sovereignty, and many may wish that more power had been given to the General Government. But this much is plain, that it is not proposed to allow anything approaching to state sovereignty here. We have not even an intelligible statement as to what powers are to be exercised by the general, and what by the local legislatures and governments. Several subjects are specifically given to both; many others are confusedly left in doubt between them; and there is the strange and anomalous provision that not only can the General Government disallow the acts of the provincial legislatures, and control and hamper and fetter provincial action in more ways than one, but that wherever any federal legislation contravenes or in any way clashes with provincial legislation, as to any matter at all common between them, such federal legislation shall override it, and take its place. It is not too much to say that a continuance of such a system for any length of time without serious clashing is absolutely impossible. This is in effect so declared in the despatch of Her Majesty's Colonial Secretary, and it is clearly pointed out in the London *Times* and in the *Edinburgh Review*. It seems as if our statesmen had sought to multiply points of collision at every turn. Then as to the non provision of a permanent seat of government, and the arrangements contemplated for the judiciary, we find still

more of the same sort of thing; and as to the extraordinary pains that seem to have been taken to throw up a great wall or hedge round those institutions of Lower Canada which of late have been giving us no trouble to speak of—as to the extraordinary pains, I say, that seem to have been taken to put a wall around those institutions, and to give every possible guarantee about them on this side and on that; why, this very machinery, provided for the mere purpose of inducing people to agree to the scheme, who would not otherwise countenance it, is calculated, at no very distant day, to cause the cry to resound throughout the land—"To your tents, O, Israel!" (Hear, hear.) I had reached this point of my argument, when I was compelled to throw myself on the indulgence of the House. There is just one consideration connected with these matters to which I have been alluding, that I wish to revert to in few words, because I believe it escaped me, in part at least, last night. A marked difference between the history of the United States just before they framed their constitution, and our late history, is this: the adoption of the Constitution of the United States followed immediately upon their successful war of independence. The men who adopted it had just gone shoulder to shoulder through the severest trial that could have been given to their patience and other higher qualities. Their entire communities had been, you may say, united as one man, in the great struggle through which they had passed, and were then equally united in their hopes as to the grand results which their new system was to bring forth. They had tried the system of mere confederation, and were agreed that it was inadequate to meet the wants of their situation. They were all trying to remove the evils that they felt and apprehended from it, and to build up a great nationality that should endure in the future. That was the position they occupied. Ours is some thing very different indeed. We have not gone through an ordeal such as that through which they had so proudly passed. On the contrary, we have ended, temporarily ended at any rate, a series of struggles it is true, but struggles of a very different kind; struggles that have just pitted our public men one against another, and to some extent, I am sorry to say, even our faiths and races against each other. (Hear, hear.) For one, I do believe that these struggles—of the latter class I mean—were dying out, but for these contemplated changes, which are threatening to revive them. But, however that may be, struggles there have been amongst us, of which we have no cause to be proud; things have occurred since the union of which we ought to be ashamed, if we are not (Hear, hear.) Of this kind are the only struggles that we have had; and when, from such a past and present, we are told to start with the idea, so to speak, of at once creating and developing the character of a new and united nation, under institutions giving us a something short of independence, and at the same time any quantity of matters about which to dispute and come to trouble, we may as well not shut our eyes to the fact, that we start with but poor omens of success. (Hear, hear.) But I have to turn now, Mr. SPEAKER, to another branch of my comparison—the financial; and here, I may at once give the House an assurance, which I am sure it will be glad to have, that I will not trouble it with more figures than are absolutely necessary to my explanation of the views I have to present, and that I will not give a single figure as to which there can be the possibility of a controversy. The contrast between the financial system as a whole, with which the framers of the United States Constitution started, and the financial system with which it is proposed we shall start, is as salient as it is possible for the human intellect to conceive; and further the contrast between this proposed financial system, and the financial system of England, is just as salient too. The framers of the United States Constitution started with the principle, that between the United States and the several states there should be no financial dealings at all. They were to have separate financial systems, separate treasuries, separate debts —all absolutely distinct. And ever since the time when the unhappy attempt on the part of Great Britain to tax the colonies was given up, almost as absolute a line of demarcation between the Imperial finances and treasury and the colonial finances and treasuries, has been maintained. We have had our own separate finances and our own separate treasury, with which the Imperial Government has had nothing to do. The Imperial Government may have gone, and may still go, to some expense on provincial behalf; but the British principle is, that Imperial finance is as distinct from the provincial, as in the United States Federal finance is from that of any state. Now, the system proposed here for our adoption is not this of entire and simple separation of the federal from the provincial treasuries, but a system of the most entire and complex confusion between them. One has to think a good deal upon the subject, and to study it pretty closely to see precisely how the confusion is going to operate; but there it is, unmistakably, at every turn. I do not mean to say that under all the circumstances of the case something of this sort was not unavoidable. In the course of debate the other day, I remember a remark was thrown across the floor of the House upon this point and the Hon. Minister of Finance in effect said: "Yes, indeed, and it would have been a very pleasant thing for gentlemen opposed to the scheme, if it had thrown upon the provinces a necessity of resorting to direct taxation." Of course, in the mere view of making the scheme palatable, it was clever to make the Federal treasury pay for provincial expenditure; but the system that had need be established should bear testimony, not to cleverness, but to wisdom. Is the system proposed for our acceptance as good, then, as statesmen ought to and would have made it? I think not; and the extraordinary thing is, that it is brought out with a flourish of trumpets, on the ground that in some undescribable way it is to work most economically! (Hear, hear.) Well, to test it, I will take it up in three points of view—first, as to assets; next, as to debts and liabilities; and, lastly, as to revenues. As to the asset part of the question, the tale is soon told. The assets of these provinces, speaking generally, are of very little commercial value. They are much like the assets of an insolvent trader, with lots of bad debts upon his books; it is of small consequence to whom or how they are assigned. The general principle upon which the scheme proceeds, is to give the Federal Government the bulk of these assets. The only exceptions of any consequence—I am not going into the details of the scheme, but still I must present to the House so much of detail as to show that I am making no rash statement, not borne out by facts—the only important exceptions, I say, to this rule are those I am about to notice. Certain properties such as penitentiaries, prisons, lunatic asylums, and other public charitable institutions, and other buildings and properties of the kind, which, together with those I have just mentioned, may be characterized as exceptional properties, are to be assigned by the general to the provincial governments.

Also, with the exception of Newfoundland, the several provinces are to take the public lands, mines, minerals and royalties in each, and all assets connected with them—in common parlance, their territorial revenues. The General Government is, however, to have the mines, minerals and public lands of Newfoundland, paying for them of course. (Hear, hear.) Then, Upper and Lower Canada are severally to have those assets which are connected with the debts, reserved for payment by them respectively; but these will not be worth much, and I shall not take the trouble of saying much about them. It is enough to know that the proportion of the debts to be assumed by the two has not yet, for some reason, been stated, and that the assets connected with them amount to very little. Further, I am not quite sure that I am right, but I understood the Hon. Attorney General for Lower Canada, the other night, to intimate that the seigniory of Sorel is to be somehow a provincial asset of Lower Canada. If that is not to be the case I will pass on ; but if it is, perhaps the honorable gentleman will say so.

Hon. Atty. Gen. CARTIER—I will speak on that subject at another time.

Mr. DUNKIN—Then, I am to take it for granted, I suppose, that it is not to be a provincial asset?

Hon. Atty. Gen. CARTIER—I will not interrupt the hon. gentleman now.

Mr. DUNKIN—Well, Mr. Speaker, I did suppose that I should have had an immediate answer as to whether this seigniory is to be a provincial asset or not; but the hon. gentleman does not seem inclined to give any information upon the point. By these resolutions it is provided, that all ordnance properties are to be taken by the General Government; and I never heard but that the seigniory of Sorel is an ordnance property. But from the statement made here the other day, it would seem that although this printed document purports to be the scheme, it does not give us true information on this point. The wording of the 55th resolution is, that the "property transferred by the Imperial Government and known as ordnance property" is to belong to the General Government; if any part of it is really a provincial asset, it must become so by one of those explanations or glosses which we are not allowed to insert in the instrument now, but are to take our chance of for some future time. (Hear, hear.) Passing over the mystery that seems to

hang over the subject, I refer then to a matter about which there can be no mistake. There certainly cannot be a doubt that the lands, mines, and minerals of Newfoundland are to be a Federal asset ; and there is not any doubt either that the Federal Government will have to pay $150,000 a year for them. It is perfectly certain that these lands will cost that money; and it is perfectly certain, I think, that the administration of them will also cost a certain amount of trouble and dispute, as to the manner in which it is to be carried on. But if human nature remains human nature, we may reasonably and probably surmise that they will not yield so great a revenue to the General Government as is by some thought. We shall have Newfoundland delegations in the Commons House, and in the other House ; and in order to keep them in anything like good humor, and to enable the Lieutenant-Governor of Newfoundland to carry on his government with anything like ease and comfort, their lands, mines and minerals will have to be administered, not with a view to Federal revenue—even though to that end they are costing the direct payment of $150,000 a year—but with a view to Newfoundland popularity. In fact, I think it will be found that the management of these properties will be carried on more with a view to the development and profit of Newfoundland, than for any profit of the people of Nova Scotia, New Brunswick, and Upper and Lower Canada. Every man, woman and child — from the Lieutenant-Governor downwards—connected with Newfoundland, will regard it as a fit article of political faith, that they must be worked with a special view to the great future of that great country. And the consequence will be many little passages between the province and the Federal Government, not advantageous to the latter, but illustrative of the way in which governments too often have to deal with things for which they have had to pay. Well, sir, I pass to the matter of the debts; and these, it must be acknowledged, are rather more important than the assets. (Hear, hear.) There is no mistake about that; though there might seem to be a mistake about the resolutions on this subject, were you to take their letter only. The sixtieth resolution says that the General Government shall assume all the debts and liabilities of each province; while the sixty-first has it, that part of our Canadian debt is to be borne by Upper and

Lower Canada respectively. In a sense, I will presently explain. I think the sixtieth resolution about tells the truth, or rather, I ought to say, falls short of it. But it requires one to work the oracle out, to follow the calculation through, in order to see that it does so, that these debts will indeed all—and more than all—fall, directly or indirectly, on the Federal Government. Meantime, on our way to that part of my argument, I set it down that under the sixty-first resolution there is an amount of reserved debt which, in a certain manner, is to fall on Upper and Lower Canada respectively. Pretty much as it was just now in the ordnance property, so here, we cannot get an intelligible answer as to what these reserved debts are, as against either province, or what the assets are that each is to take as an offset to them. But, for the purpose of constituting the stated debt of the future Confederation, Upper and Lower Canada, we are told, are to throw into it an amount of $62,500,000, the surplus of their debt being nominally left to be borne by themselves, after they shall have become confederated; Nova Scotia, on the other hand, is to be allowed to increase her debt to $8,000,000; and Newfoundland and Prince Edward Island are to throw in theirs at the nominal figure they stand at now. But, by an ingenious contrivance, the aggregate real debt of the country is to be, in effect, a good deal more than the aggregation of those figures would give. Upper and Lower Canada, to begin with, as we have seen, are, besides, separately to pretend to bear the weight of their considerable excess of debt over the $62,500,000, or $25 a head, allowed under this arrangement. Nova Scotia and New Brunswick, should they not increase their debts to be assumed up to this figure of $25 a head, are to be paid interest at five per cent. on any amount of shortcoming in that behalf they may be guilty of. And Newfoundland and Prince Edward Island are to be paid interest at the same rate, on the amount to which their smaller debts fall short of this same normal $25 allowance. For practical purposes, therefore, the debts of the four Lower Provinces are thus brought up to this standard level. The Federal Government is to pay interest on them to that tune—if not to creditors of those provinces, then to the provinces themselve. And we are to start with a clear, practical debt of $25 a head for every man, woman, and child in the Confederacy. Incurred or not, we start with it as due, and pay accordingly. And there are, besides, those amounts of debt left nominally to the charge of Upper Canada, as to which I shall have a word more to say shortly. Meantime, I proceed to our third head—of revenues. And here, the first and most striking fact is, that the Federal Government is to make yearly grants, payable, by the way, semi-annually and in advance, to each province, in proportion to its population as shown by the census of 1861, and at the rate of 80 cents a head. And the way in which this 80 cents a head apportionment is come at, is in itself somewhat edifying. According to the statements made here by Ministers, the Finance Ministers of the several provinces were invited at the Conference to come forward with a statement of their respective wants. Of course their statements were to be framed with a due regard to economy. Such things are always to be done economically. This is a diplomatic phrase, of which we understand here the full meaning; and I was not at all surprised to hear, that however economically the statements were made out, they had to be cut down. Whether they are said to have been cut down once or twice, or oftener, I do not distinctly recollect. But at last, after having been duly cut down, they were found to require this grant or subvention, at the rate of 80 cents a head all round—subject always to deduction as against the Canadas, and to additions in favor of the four Lower Provinces, as we shall presently see. With less, the provinces could not get on at the rate thought necessary, unless by levying undesired taxes. Well, besides these subventions, the provinces (all but Newfoundland) are to have the proceeds of their lands, mines and minerals; and Newfoundland is to have, instead, the further grant from the Federal treasury, of $150,000 a year, for ever. They may all, further, derive some more indirect revenue from licenses of various sorts; and Nova Scotia may add to these an exceptional, and exceptionable, export duty on coal and other minerals; and New Brunswick, the like on lumber. Besides which, on the mere ground that she cannot do without it, New Brunswick is to have a further Federal grant of $63,000 a year for ten years; unless, indeed, in the event of her not augmenting her debt to the full amount, in which case, any payment made to her of interest on that score is to be deducted from the $63,000—a shrewd hint, by the way, that she had not best be too economical—and, lastly, all are to have the precious right of direct taxation, and the higher privilege of borrowing without limit. The Federal power is to have, of course, the right to tax in all sorts of ways, the special export duties made over to New Brunswick and Nova Scotia, alone excepted. Now, Mr. SPEAKER, taking this whole arrangement together, I must repeat that I see in it no principle but one. The provinces are to be able to carry on their operations according to their supposed probable future exigencies, without danger of direct, that is to say, oppressive or new taxation. Well, sir, engineers say that the measure of strength of a fortified place is the strength of its weakest part. And this principle is here applied to our provinces in a financial point of view. The need of the neediest is made the measure of the aid given to all. The most embarrassed is to have enough for its purposes, and the rest are to receive, if not exactly in the same ratio, at least so nearly up to the mark as that they shall all be satisfied; while, on the other hand, the debts of all the provinces are to be, for all practical ends, raised to the full level of the most indebted. To show this, sir, another word or two as to the amount of the promised subventions to Upper and Lower Canada. This is to be, as we have seen, only the 80 cents a head, less some deduction, I care not what, for the purpose of my present argument; but there is no doubt, I say, that they are to receive less than the 80 cents, because the excess of their debt over $62,-500,000, though thrown on them, will have to be guaranteed, and the interest on it will have be paid by the Federal Government, and that interest will be deducted by the Federal Government from the subventions payable to them respectively. The Lower Provinces, on the other hand, as we have also seen, are really to get more. Well now, suppose for the moment the arrangement had been, for the Confederation to assume at once the whole debt of Canada, and accordingly to pay proportionably larger amounts of interest to the other provinces. The two Canadas would then have needed, exactly, so much the less of nominal subvention, and the other provinces too. The cost to the Federal treasury, in the whole, would still have been exactly what it is. Indirectly, therefore, I say that for all practical purposes there is thrown upon the General Government the whole amount of the past debts of these provinces, and more;

and the whole burden, too, of the carrying on of the machinery of government, both Federal and Provincial; unless, indeed, any of the provinces should see fit hereafter to undertake what I may call extraordinary expenditure, and to defray it themselves. I do not think they will. It would involve direct taxation. And I think they can do better. But for all this part of the plan, sir, it is like the rest, framed on the mere idea of making things pleasant—the politician idea of anyhow winning over interests or parties for to-day—not on any statesmanlike thought as to its future working and effects. (Hear, hear.) Now, Mr. SPEAKER, with this outline of the system, I should be glad to know where the prospect of economy of administration is to be found. The Honorable Finance Minister of the future Federal Government will have to do—what? To come with a budget, not merely to cover the outlay of the Federal Government—that is of course—but with a budget to cover also all that I may call the normal outlay, the intended outlay, the foreseen outlay of all the provinces. (Hear, hear.) The Minister of Finance—if any there is—of the province, unless he chooses to outrun the constable; unless, with his lieutenant-governor and local government and legislature, he chooses to spend more than he can get out of the Federal Government, by this system, or by that nice modification of it which is pretty sure to be soon thought of, and to which I shall by and by advert, need have no budget at all. He knows he is to have about so much from his lands, mines and minerals, so much from licenses and so forth, so much from the Federal Government, so many thousand or hundred thousand dollars in all; and he will of course make the best he can of that. And by the way, it is a remarkable fact in this connection, that we find that with one accord those who are undertaking to speak to the different provinces in support of Confederation are agreed in each telling the people of his own province what a first-rate bargain has been made for it. (Hear, hear.) My hon. friend from Hochelaga read us an extract the other night from a speech of Hon. Mr. TILLEY, of New Brunswick, in which that hon. gentleman cyphered out, perfectly to his satisfaction, and to that of many who heard him, that New Brunswick is guaranteed an excess over her real needs, of $34,000 a year. If I am not mistaken, the Hon. Solicitor General for Lower Canada undertook since, in this House, to shew us that some $200,000 or more a-

year beyond hers, is in the same way secured
to Lower Canada ; even though she does
not receive the full 80 cents a head. I
think I remember that the Hon. President of
the Council—though I have not yet got the
report of his speech to refresh my memory—
made it a point that really Upper Canada,
as well as Lower Canada, is comfortably off
in this respect. One hears too, I think, of
the same song in Nova Scotia ; and in Prince
Edward Island certainly, we have the advocates of Confederation telling the people
there—" You, too, have got a capital bargain,
you have so much more to spend, according
to this arrangement, than you ever had before."
A strange comment on that earnest desire for
economy, which is claimed to have dictated
the whole of these arrangements. (Hear,
hear.) If that was the intention, the per-
formance has fallen far short of it. (Hear,
hear.) And before I go further, there
occurs to me this consideration, arising out
of this state of things—out of this abundance, not to say plethora, that is meant to
characterize the provincial exchequers, whatever may be the case with the Federal
exchequer under the system—one consideration, I say, connected with this, which should
not be lost sight of when we are talking about
the application of anything in the least like
responsible government to our provinces. I
never yet heard of an elected legislative body
that had much control over a government,
unless it had hold of the strings of a purse
from which the government wanted to get
something. In the old days, before responsible government was thought of—in the days
when casual and territorial revenues gave
provincial governments all they wanted, or a
little more—provincial legislatures had mighty
little to do with government, and, if they
complained of a grievance, were little likely
to be listened to? It was even the same long
before at home. When the English Crown
had its abundance of resources, English kings
cared little for their parliaments. But when
their resources were exhausted, and they could
not borrow easily, and had to ask for taxes,
then the House of Commons began to acquire
power, and, in course of time, became the
body it is now. I shall be surprised if we do
not find, in the event of this Confederation
taking place, that for some time our provincial legislatures, whether they consist of
one chamber or of two, will be less powerful
for good than many would wish to have
them, that the machine of state will not be
altogether driven by their means. But there
is another result, about which there can

be no question. With one accord, not in
Newfoundland merely—I was hinting a little
while ago at what would be the case of
Newfoundland, as to its lands, mines and
minerals—not there only, but in all the provinces—the provincial governments will, in
a quiet way, want money, and the provincial
legislators and people will want it yet more ;
grants for roads and bridges, for schools, for
charities, for salaries, for contingencies of the
legislative body—for all manner of ends they
will be wanting money, and where is it to
come from ? Whether the constitution of
the Provincial Executive savors at all of responsible government or not, be sure it will
not be anxious to bring itself more under the
control of the legislature, or to make itself
more odious than it can help, and the easiest
way for it to get money will be from the General Government. I am not sure, either, but
that most members of the provincial legislatures will like it that way the best. (Hear,
hear.) It will not be at all unpopular,
the getting of money so. Quite the contrary.
Gentlemen will go to their constituents with
an easy conscience, telling them : " True, we
had not much to do in the Provincial Legislature, and you need not ask very closely
what else we did ; but I tell you what, we
got the Federal Government to increase the
subvention to our province by five cents a
head, and see what this gives you—$500 to
that road—$1000 to that charity—so much
here, so much there. That we have done ;
and have we not done well ?" (Hear, hear.)
I am afraid in many constituencies the answer would be; " Yes, you have done well ;
go and do it again." I am afraid the provincial constituencies, legislatures and executives
will all show a most calf-like appetite for the
milking of this one most magnificent government cow.

HON. J. S. MACDONALD—There will
be more municipal loan funds.

MR. DUNKIN—Yes, that is one of the
analogies, and there is another even nearer.
Years ago, we in Canada said we would for ever
give a certain fixed sum per annum for an education fund. It was to be divided, in a certain ratio, between Upper and Lower Canada.
But from time to time, as the census shewed
changes of their relative population, the division was to be altered. In a little while this
alteration of ratio gave Lower Canada less
money and Upper Canada more. "Oh! but,"
said the Administration, "we cannot do that
with Lower Canada. After having had distributed to her so many thousands a year, she could
not stand having ever so much less. No, no;

we cannot do that. What shall we do, then? In our estimates we will put in a vote for Lower Canada, just to keep her figure up to the mark of what she has been receiving. And what then? Why, of course, we must add a vote for Upper Canada in the same proportion, just to take her so much further beyond her former figure." (Hear, hear.) To be sure, I do find, with reference to this subvention, a pleasant little expression, which one wishes may be carried out. It is to be " in full." " Such aid shall be in *full settlement* of all future demands upon the General Government for local purposes, and shall be paid half-yearly, in advance, to each province." Yes, sir, so the text runs. But suppose ourselves in the time of our first, or second, or third Federal Cabinet, consisting of its six or more sections, of course; and, for the sake of my argument, I will suppose a great deal, that every one of these sections controls comfortably the delegations from its own province in the two Houses of Parliament, that the machine is working beautifully, that there is no lieutenant-governor crusty, no provincial administration kicking over the traces, and no provincial legislature giving any other trouble than by its anxiety to be well paid. I will suppose even that this halcyon state of things has gone on for some time. But one or two or more of the provinces begin to feel that they cannot do without having more money. And the pressure will be such upon the Provincial Legislature and upon the Lieutenant-Governor, and upon the delegations to the General Legislature, and upon the section of the Federal Executive representing each such province, that it never can be long resisted; there will be trouble if it is, and things must be kept pleasant. (Hear, hear.) One mode—the most obvious, though the least scientific—will be just to increase the subvention from eighty to eighty-five, or even to eighty-two or eighty-one cents a head. An additional cent a head from the Federal Exchequer would be an object—a few cents a head would be a boon. Or suppose the demand took this form : suppose the people —say of Upper or Lower Canada—should say, " Those Newfoundlanders are getting $150,000 a year for their lands, mines, and minerals; and the Federal Government is positively administering those lands, mines, and minerals, not for Federal profit, but more for the advantage of that province than we find we can administer our own; the General Government, therefore, must take our lands, mines, and minerals, and give us also an equivalent." That is one way of doing the

thing; and, when the time comes for making that sort of demand, depend upon it that it will sound singularly reasonable in the ears of the provinces whose representatives shall make it; and if two or three provinces shall join in the demand, my word for it, the thing will soon be done. The same sort of thing may be looked for in reference to the New Brunswick timber export duty and the Nova Scotia mineral export duty. Here is one form of the cry that may be raised—" You give these exceptional privileges to New Brunswick and Nova Scotia; give them, or some equivalent, to us also." With common ingenuity lots of such cries may be nicely got up. But for everything so given, much or little, to whatever province, you will have to do the like for all the rest, and the figure will be alarming before you get to the end. And even this is not all. Not only will you have these comparatively direct demands—more or less ingeniously, but always irresistibly—made, but you will have demands made in a more indirect form which it will be yet easier to carry, from their consequences not being so clearly seen, and which will therefore be still worse in their effects. I speak of that tremendous catalogue of outlays which may be gone into without the appearance of a grant to any particular province—the costly favors which may be done in respect of inter-provincial ferries, steamship lines between or from the provinces, railways between or through the provinces, telegraph lines, agriculture, immigration, quarantine, fisheries, and so forth. There will be claims of every description under all these heads; and besides them there will be the long roll of internal improvements of all kinds, whether for the benefit of one or of more than one of the provinces. For any local work in which it can be at all pretended that it is of general interest, pressure may be brought to bear upon the General Government and Legislature, and whenever one province succeeds in getting any such grant, every other province must be dealt with in the same way. Compensation must be made all round, and no human intellect can estimate the degree of extravagance that before long must become simply inevitable. (Hear, hear.) Sir, with our Upper and Lower Canada we have had pretty good proof of this. We know that whenever anything has had to be done for one section of this province, it has constantly been found necessary to do something of the same or of some other kind for the other. If either needed anything very badly, then the ingenuity of the Minister of Finance had to be exercised to discover something else of like value to give the other. In one word, unless I am more mistaken than I think I can be, these local governments will be pretty good daughters of the horse-leech, and their cry will be found to be pretty often and pretty successfully—" Give, give, give!" But, sir, there is very little need for our dealing with considerations of this kind as to a future about which one may be thought to be in danger of drawing more or less upon imagination. We have in these resolutions a something that is to come upon us, one may say, at once; I allude to the expenditure for our defences—the Intercolonial Railway—the opening of communication with the North-West—and the enlargement of our canals. There is no doubt that all these new sources of outlay are immediately contemplated. Their cost is not given us; it could not be given with any safety to the scheme. I do not pretend to say, sir, but that some of these expenditures are necessary; and this I am even prepared to say as to one of them — the outlay for defences—that every province of the empire is bound to do its full share towards its own defence. (Hear, hear.) I never gave a vote or expressed an opinion in any other sense. I was always ready with my vote for that purpose. (Hear, hear.) But looking at the great outlay, I may say the enormous outlay here understood to be contemplated, I confess I cannot approach the subject in this connection without a feeling of misgiving. I can quite understand our going to the full limit of our means for all the expense that is necessary for the thorough maintenance of our militia on an efficient footing as to instruction and otherwise; but when we hear of Imperial engineers, with Imperial ideas as to cost, laying out grand permanent works of defence, then I confess I am much inclined to think that we had need try to practice what economy we can in that direction. (Hear, hear.) Then, as regards the Intercolonial Railway, we have in these resolutions a very blind tale indeed. "The General Government shall secure, without delay, the completion of the Intercolonial Railway from Rivière du Loup, through New Brunswick, to Truro in Nova Scotia"—and this quite irrespectively of the expense. The vague pledge is, that the General Government shall at any cost secure the immediate completion of this work. As to its commercial or military advantages, I have not a great idea of them. I believe there has been much exaggeration as to both. Unless with a strong force to defend it, in a military point of view, it would be of just no use at all. (Hear, hear.)

6

For my own part, as I have often said, I heartily wish to see the road built; but unless we can get it done upon terms within our means, we had better do without it a little longer, and develope what other means of communication are at our command. While I want to see the thing done, I am not prepared for the declaration I find in these resolutions, that, coûte que coûte, we will at once have it. I doubt the policy of that way of dealing. (Hear, hear.) Viewed in its political aspects, the work is as much an Imperial as a provincial work; is one for which we have a right to look for aid from the Empire. I know it is said the Empire is going to aid us. Well, for a long time we held this language: if the Imperial Government and the Lower Provinces between them will combine to do the rest, we are ready with lands and subsidies, in a certain proportion and to a certain limited amount. It is unfortunate, in my opinion, that that proposal led to no result. I should have been glad to have obtained it on such terms, and even would have bid up the limit to the utmost extent of our means.

Hon. J. S. MACDONALD—That offer is extant yet.

Mr. DUNKIN—I know it is, but those since made have left it out of sight. In 1862 the start was made to a larger and not limited outlay—five-twelfths of an unstated whole— Great Britain to reduce the cost by endorsing for us to a stated figure. I regretted that scheme; but still it was better for us than what is now being forced upon us. By this last scheme, Canada will have to bear some nine-twelfths—it has been said ten-twelfths— but some nine-twelfths, at any rate. In fact, the bulk of the burden is to fall on us; and it is significant, though I dare say that the honorable gentlemen who drew up this resolution did not mean it, that it seems to let the Imperial Government off from its guarantee. This is no mere criticism of mine; my attention was drawn to the point by the article in the *Edinburgh Review* from which I was quoting last night. That writer—who is not a nobody, you may depend upon it—remarks, in effect, that from the wording of this resolution, the honorable gentlemen of the Conference do not seem to be holding to the Imperial guarantee. Should it not be given, the cost to us will be frightfully increased. And this it had not need be. For the honorable gentlemen who are running us into it might do well to remember the past. We had the Grand Trunk railway offered us for what was called next to nothing. The guarantee we were to give was not for much; and it was well secured; and we were assured it was not meant to be made use of—was more a form than a reality. Yet the guarantee was used and extended, and made a gift of; every estimate failed ; the cry ever since has been for more, more ; and the whole concern is now in such a state as to be threatening us day by day with yet larger demands on the public purse than ever, to keep it going. Well, sir, I pass on from these heavy outlays for permanent defences, and the Intercolonial Railway ; and I read in these resolutions that " the communications with the North-Western territory, and the improvements required for the development of the trade of the Great West with the seaboard, are regarded by this Conference as subjects of the highest importance to the Federated Provinces, and shall be prosecuted at the earliest possible period that the state of the finances will permit." Well, sir, we are told that this last phrase is synonymous with those unqualified words, "without delay," that are used as to the Intercolonial. I am reminded of a saying current in the days of Lord SYDENHAM, who was a good deal in the habit of wanting work done faster than the workers liked, and of whom it used to be said that all he ordered had to be done "immediately, if not sooner." (Hear, hear, and laughter.) I take it, the Intercolonial Railway is to be done " immediately, if not sooner," and these other improvements are to wait till "immediately, if not later." They are to be prosecuted as soon as the state of the finances will permit. I know some hon. gentlemen think that will be very soon, but if so, there must be most extraordinary means taken to borrow or otherwise raise money. (Hear, hear.) Nothing can be vaguer than the intimation given as to what these works are to be. The communications with the Great North-Western territory, where are they to begin; what are they to be; and where are they to end? And the other improvements to be carried out—the communications with the seaboard—the enlargement of the canals—how much enlargement, sir, and of how many and what canals? An honorable friend near me says canal enlargement is or should be productive. No doubt, but at what rate? I remember reading in a Lower Province paper the other day of a late speech of Hon. Mr. TILLEY'S, in which he said that at the Quebec Conference they went into a calculation of the productive value of the entire outlay of these provinces upon productive public works,

and found them to be yielding an average of one and an eighth of one per cent., or something like that, of yearly return upon their cost. I admit there may be in the widening of these canals a something of productiveness; but to say that it will be anything like proportionate to the outlay, is absurd. But what I am coming back to is this—we are to go at once into the outlay of the Intercolonial Railway, and we are to go into this other, too; but yet, almost beyond the shadow of a doubt, these canals and other communications with the west—which western politicians think they are to get as their equivalent —are to be held back a bit. I forgot to bring here an extract from a late speech of Hon. Mr. TILLEY's, in which he plainly said that an immediate carrying on of these western works did not enter into the calculations of the Conference, that the Intercolonial was unmistakably to be put through at once; but that the Lower Province delegates gave no promise of the like prosecution of these other works as the price of that. (Hear, hear.)

AN HON. MEMBER—Where do you find that ?

MR. DUNKIN—It is quoted in a late number of the Toronto *Leader;* and if any-one will bring me the fyle of that paper from below, I will read the words with pleasure. Now, Mr. SPEAKER, I am raising no question of any one's sincerity upon this question. The politicians of the eastern provinces, I have no doubt, are thoroughly in earnest in their demand for the construction of the Intercolonial road, and are quite willing to have the western improvements begun about as soon as they can be ; and I am quite sure that the friends of this scheme in the west want their western works instantly gone on with. I even believe they both think they will get what they want; but I am surprised at their credulity, for I do not see how they can. I believe they are deceiving themselves and their friends with the bright pictures their fancy has been painting, and that my western friends, at any rate, are doomed to some disappointment. Whenever a Federal Parliament shall meet, I fancy it will become a question of grave interest whether or not the state of the finances will admit of the construction of all these works ; and if not, then what is to be done first—and how— and when ? And as I have shewn, unless the six majorities are pretty much agreed, there will be no great deal done in any hurry·

HON. J. S. MACDONALD—That is worse than the double majority.

Mr. DUNKIN—Yes, three times as bad, to say the least. Well, suppose the financiers of the Lower Provinces, having before their eyes the fear of direct taxation by the Federal Parliament, should come to the conclusion that it will not signify for a few years, whether these western works are begun at once or not; and should propose to sit down first a little, and count the cost.

Hon. J. S. MACDONALD—Insist on having a survey made, for instance, first?

Mr. DUNKIN—Well yes, that would probably be insisted upon before they would consent to commit themselves further to the undertaking. Suppose, then, Lower Canada to go with the Lower Provinces for staving off this commencement of these works, how will it fare with Upper Canada's demand for them? And what will not be the indignation of the people of Upper Canada at being tied to, and controlled by the non-progressive people of the east? Or, suppose that Upper and Lower Canada should agree, and the Lower Provinces be seriously angry, at any over-caution eastward, or over-rashness westward; would not they too, so left out in the cold, be making things quite unpleasant? Or again, suppose the more eastern and the western interests should continue to push on both plans, careless of cost, and that Lower Canada, for fear of direct taxation, should hold back in earnest, would that make no trouble? Is not any one of these suppositions more probable than the cool assumption, over which western gentlemen are so happy, that when the time comes all interests will instantly work together, and by magic do everything, east and west, at once? But, be this as it may, sir, on all three accounts—defences, Intercolonial road and western works—we are sure of cost, as well as of disputes, in plenty. And there is, besides, a fourth. I shall have occasion to shew presently that we are going to be called upon to spend money for yet another kindred purpose, and a large amount too—and this, as a part of this scheme. Our star of empire is to wing its way westward; and we are to confederate everything in its track, from Newfoundland to Vancouver's Island, this last included. But, between us and it, there lies the Hudson Bay territory. So, of course, we must acquire that for confederation purposes; and the plan is, that before we get it we shall have to pay for the elephant—though, after we get him, we may find him costly and hard to keep. It will not be difficult to prove that this is

contemplated by the promoters of this scheme. Between railways and canals, and western extension, before we get the scheme carried out in all its contemplated amplitude, we shall have bled pretty well, and seen some sights that we have hardly yet learnt to anticipate. (Hear, hear.) Well, with this certain prospect before us of a gigantic outlay, what is the prospect for a gigantic income?

A MEMBER—Oh, never mind that.

Mr. DUNKIN—I quite understand that many hon. gentlemen take little thought of where money is to come from, if only it is to be spent as they wish. But, Mr. SPEAKER, before I go further, I am handed the fyle of the Toronto Leader, and, with the leave of the House, I will read from it the extracts from Hon. Mr. TILLEY's speech to which I was referring some minutes ago. This journal refers to it as follows:—

Mr. TILLEY, we are sorry to say, does not give us much hope of the speedy enlargement of our canals. He laughs at the idea of his opponent quoting Mr. BROWN as authority that this work is to be undertaken at once. "The Conference," says Mr. TILLEY, "agreed to build the railroad without delay, the canals as soon as the state of the finances will permit." But he ridicules the idea that the finances will be held at once to admit of this being done. "Canada," says Mr. TILLEY, "could not have been brought into the union on a promise to build her canals, for the railroad will cost $12,000,000, which added to the $22,000,000 for canals, would be an amount far above what they could have gained them for without Confederation."

Such is Hon. Mr. TILLEY's style of remark, and I do not think it is at all encouraging to the very sanguine view of the scheme taken by some western politicians. It is presumable that he will take Newfoundland, Prince Edward Island and Nova Scotia with him, and along with them he will get much of Lower Canada. If I should have the honor of a seat in the House, they may depend upon it, I shall do what I can to get them fair play. But I repeat, I do not expect to see them satisfied with the result. Well, sir, however this may be, there is going to be, at any rate, an immense amount of money required, come from whence it may. Where is it to come from? We cannot shut our eyes to the fact, that the customs tariff must come down. (Hear.) There are no two ways about that. Our tariff is much higher than those of the Lower Provinces; and the advocates of Confederation there have to assure people that their tariffs will not be materially raised, in order to get any sort of hearing for the scheme. To tell them that the tariff of Canada is to be that of the Confederation, would be to ruin the chances of getting a favorable reception for it. (Hear, hear.) We are marching fast and steadily towards free trade. We must meet the views of the people of the Lower Provinces, who are hostile to high tariffs, and the demand of the Imperial authorities that we should not tax their manufactures so heavily as—in their phrase—almost to deprive them of our market. It was distinctly and officially stated the other day, in Newfoundland, that assurance had been given to the Government of Newfoundland that the views of the Canadian Government are unmistakably in this direction. And I do not think there is any mistake about that, either. To shew how people at home, too, expect our tariff to come down, I may refer to the speech of Mr. HAMBURY TRACY, in seconding the Address in answer to the Speech from the Throne, in the House of Commons the other day. He could not stop, after saying generally that he was pleased with this Confederation movement, without adding that he trusted it would result in a very considerable decrease in the absurdly high and hostile tariff at present prevailing in Canada. I have not here the exact words, but that was their purport. Well, if the customs tariff is to come down largely, we must look for a decrease of revenue. I am free to admit that a reduction of the tariff on certain articles, or even some measure of reduction all round, might be no material loss, or might even be a gain, to the revenue— in ordinary or prosperous times, that is to say. But when the object of reducing the tariff is to meet other exigencies than those of revenue, one can hardly hope to get such a tariff as shall give us the largest revenue attainable. And besides, no one can deny that we are about entering upon a time, commercially speaking, that may be termed hard. We have had, for some time past, pretty heavy importations, and our best informed and shrewdest commercial men tell us that we are going to have, for some time to come, pretty light importations. We are not to have a plethoric purse, even under ordinary drafts upon it, for some years.

Hon. Mr. HOLTON—The hard time is come now.

Mr. DUNKIN—Yes, it is come, or is close on us, and it rather threatens to last. And if, with this state of things before us, to oblige the Imperial authorities and the Lower Provinces, under pressure of an inevitable state necessity, we are to reduce our customs rates, or any number of them, below what I may call their figure of largest productiveness, then surely it is little to say that we cannot look forward to an increase in the revenue, or even to a continuance of our present income, and it is rather strange that we should be called upon, withal, at the same time so to change our whole system as to involve ourselves in the enormous extravagances here contemplated. No taxing scheme can ever meet the case. Nothing can be looked to, but a device of borrowing without limit—the incurring of an amount of debt that, in interest and sinking fund, must prove to be simply unendurable hereafter. (Hear, hear.) But, in fact, we cannot even borrow to any large amount unless under false pretences. We cannot borrow without telling tales of our condition, resources and expectations, that will in the end be found out to be lies. We must awaken hopes in the minds of money lenders abroad, that cannot but prove delusive—the memory of which must work us hereafter an aggravation of punishment that we shall then scarcely need. And when that time of reckoning shall have come, then staggering under the load, without credit at home or abroad, the country will have to choose whether it will have heavy direct taxation—for heavy such taxation then must be —or have recourse to more or less of repudiation; or even run some risk of both. Sir, if ever that time shall come, the public men of that day and the people on whom the burthen will then press, will not bless the memory of those who held out the false hopes and inducements under which it is now sought to decoy us into wild expenditure and crushing debt. (Hear, hear.) Well, Mr. SPEAKER, I now pass to another branch of my subject altogether. There is a further salient contrast between the American system and the system proposed for our adoption. The people of the United States, when they adopted their Constitution, were one of the nations of the earth. They formed their whole system with a view to national existence. They had fought for their independence, and had triumphed; and still in the flush of their triumph, they were laying the foundations of a system absolutely national. Their Federal Government was to have its relations with other nations, and was sure to have plenty to do upon entering the great family of nations. But we—what are we doing? Creating a new nationality, according to the advocates of this scheme. I hardly know whether we are to take the phrase for ironical, or not. Is it a reminder that in fact we have no sort of nationality about us, but are unpleasantly cut up into a lot of struggling nationalities, as between ourselves? Unlike the people of the United States, we are to have no foreign relations to look after, or national affairs of any kind; and therefore our new nationality, if we could create it, could be nothing but a name. I must say that according to my view of the change we ought to aim at, any idea of Federation that we may entertain had need take an Imperial direction. Whenever changing our institutions, we had need develope and strengthen—not merely maintain, but maintain, develope and strengthen—the tie, not yet Federal as it ought to be, between us and the parent state. (Hear, hear.) It is the entire Empire that should be federalized, and cemented together as one, and not any more limited number of its dependencies here or there. A general, or so called federal government, such as we are here proposing to create, will most certainly be in a false position. As I said just now, the Federal Government of the United States was to take its place in the great family of the nations of the earth; but what place in that family are we to occupy? Simply none. The Imperial Government will be the head of the Empire as much as ever, and will alone have to attend to all foreign relations and national matters; while we shall be nothing more than we are now. Half-a-dozen colonies federated are but a federated colony after all. Instead of being so many separate provinces with workable institutions, we are to be one province most cumbrously organised—nothing more. How many grades of government are we going to have under this system? The Imperial Government, the one great head of the Empire; then this Federal Government; then our lot of provincial governments; below them again, our county municipalities, and, still below these, our township and other local municipalities. (Hear, hear.) We have thus five different sets of governmental machinery, and of these five there is just one too many in my judgment. You might as well make six while you are about it, and interpolate between our provincial and county governments a district governmental machinery. If we did that we should be doing a thing not a whit more absurd than we propose to do now, in erecting a new piece of such machinery between the Imperial and provincial governments. We do not want a third municipal government, because there is nothing for it to do; and when we propose to create a Federal Government between the Imperial and Provincial, we are equally proposing to create a something which, having nothing of its own to do, must find work by encroaching on the functions of the Imperial and provincial governments in turn, with no place among nations, no relations with other countries, no foreign policy; it will stand in just the same position towards the Imperial Government as Canada now stands in, or as Upper or Lower Canada before the union used to occupy. That intermediate work of government which is now done by the Povince of Canada, the Province of New Brunswick, the Province of Nova Scotia, the Province of Prince Edward Island and the Province of Newfoundland, is to be done, part by the Federal Government and part by the provinces. The work is simply divided that is now done by the provincial legislatures and governments, and in my opinion there is no use in this subdivision of work at all. You are putting this fifth wheel to the coach, merely to find out that a misfitting odd wheel will not serve any useful purpose, nor so much as work smoothly with the other four. (Hear, hear.) Your Federal Government will occupy about as anomalous a position between the Imperial and provincial governments as I showed, last night, will be occupied by your lieutenant governors between the Federal authority and the provinces. Both will be out of place, and to find themselves in work they must give trouble. I do not see how they can do good, but I do see how they can do any quantity of harm. (Hear, hear.) The real difficulty in our position is one that is not met by the machinery here proposed. What is that difficulty? In the larger provinces of the empire we have the system of responsible government thoroughly accorded by the Imperial Government, and thoroughly worked out; and the difficulty of the system that is now pressing, or ought to be, upon the attention of our statesmen is just this—that the tie connecting us with the Empire, and which ought to be a federal tie of the strongest kind, is too slight, is not, properly speaking, so much as a federal tie at all. These provinces, with local responsible government, are too nearly in the position of independent communities; there is not enough of connection between them and the parent state to make the relations between the two work well, or give promise of lasting long. There is in the machinery too much of what may be called the centrifugal tendency. (Hear, hear.) All the great provinces are flying off too much, attending too exclusively to mere local considerations, too little to those of the general or Imperial kind. And at home, as we seem to be flying off, they, too, are thinking of us and of the interests they and we have in common less and less. What is wanting, if one is to look to the interest of the Empire, which is really that of all its parts—what is wanting, as I have said, is an effective federalization of the Empire as a whole, not a subordinate federation here or there, made up out of parts of it. I have neither time nor strength to-night to go fairly into the question of how this thing should be done ; but a few words more as to that, I must be pardoned for. Until latterly in Canada we have not had, and some colonies have not now, I believe, a Minister of Militia. Even we have not as yet, in our Cabinet, a minister to attend to what may be called Imperial affairs. It is not the business of any minister, nor is it even distinctly recognized as that of the Ministry as a whole, in any of these provinces, to attend to what is really at the present juncture the most important part of our whole public business—the regulation of affairs between them and the Mother Country. I know it may be said this is in the hands of the Governor. So are other things. But for them, we see the need of his having advisers. And as to this, if a Cabinet leaves it wholly to him, that practically amounts to its neglecting these affairs altogether. Let me go back to a point or two in the history of affairs in Canada within the recollection of all honorable gentlemen. In 1862, when the then Militia Bill was before the House, it was asked over and over again by gentlemen of the Opposition, what communications, if any, had been received from the Imperial Government in respect of the defence of this province; and the answer invariably was, that there had been none, none known to the Administration, as an administration. Now, if there had then been an officer—the Provincial Secretary, the Minister of Militia, or any other member of the Government—whose duty it had been and was to attend to that important branch of the public service; if the relations between the Mother Country and this province had been known to be in his charge, such an answer as that could never have been given, nor the second reading of that bill lost in consequence. The other night,

when the Raid Prevention and Alien Bill was before the House, we did receive the intimation that the Mother Country desired legislation of that kind at our hands; and it passed accordingly. But that intimation was then given us exceptionally. There is a large class of questions springing up continually which affect Imperial interests and Imperial views as well as our own, and we ought to have—and if our connection with the Empire is to last, we must have—this department of our public affairs attended to by a regularly appointed Minister of the Crown here, who, whenever occasion requires, may explain them and who shall be responsible to this House. Of course, nobody denies that the Governor General is the channel of communication between us and the Imperial Government. He is the Queen's representative and servant, and his communications with the Home Government must be of the most confidential character, except in so far as he may see fit to make them known. But fully admitting this, still besides those communications of this character which he may, have and indeed at all times must have unrestrictedly with the Imperial Government, there should be —and, if our Imperial relations are to be maintained, there must be—a further class of communications between the two governments, as to which the Governor should be advised by a minister whose particular duty it should be to manage affairs between the Mother Country and ourselves, and to be in effect a local adviser, as to such matters, of the Imperial advisers of the Crown in England. In one word, we have got to develope the Imperial phase, so to speak, of our provincial system ; to find the means of keeping our policy and that of the Mother Country in harmony; and if we do not, we cannot long keep up our connection with the Empire. If this were done— if we had in our several provincial administrations some member charged with this department of the public service, as latterly we have come to have one charged with the cognate subject of the militia and defence of the country—if these ministers of Imperial relations made periodical visits home, so as there to meet one another and such members of the Imperial Government or others as the Crown might charge to meet and confer with them—if there were thus organized, some sort of advisory colonial council upon the precedent (so far, of course, as the analogy might hold) of the Council for East Indian Affairs lately created—if, I say, something in this way were done, then indeed we should be developing our Imperial relations in the proper direction, taking at least a step—the first and hardest—towards the framing of that Imperial federation of which we so stand in need. But there is no provision of that kind in the system here proposed; there is no apparent contemplation of a step of that kind in connection with this step. On the contrary, this step is all in the wrong direction. We are here proposing to create in this part of the Queen's dominions a mere sub-federation, so to speak, tending, so far as it tends to anything, towards the exclusion of this kind of provision. This other machinery to which I have been alluding, Mr. SPEAKER, if we had had it a few years ago, would have been of extreme usefulness. Suppose we had had something of that kind when the Rebellion Losses Bill was passed, when so much excitement was thereby created in the country. Suppose that then when the indignation of a large class was concentrating itself against Lord ELGIN for his supposed purpose of assenting to that bill, he could have said—"It is idle for you, as you must see, to require me to listen to you against the advice of my constitutional advisers; but you know there is a tribunal at home, to which you may appeal from that advice, where you will be heard and they, and from which you may be sure of justice if you have been aggrieved or injured here." Sir, if it had been possible for the Governor General to have given such an answer at that time to the angry remonstrances of those who opposed that measure, the Parliament House would not have been burnt, nor would we have had to deplore the long train of consequent disturbances and troubles which then and ever since have brought so much discredit and mischief to the country. Take another case. If such machinery had existed when the fishery treaty with France was entered into by the Imperial Government, conditioned upon the consent of Newfoundland, no such anomalous proceeding could have taken place. For the representatives of Newfoundland and of the rest of these provinces would at once have shown the Imperial Government that it would not meet approval in that colony, nor indeed for that matter, anywhere else in British America. Great Britain would have been saved from entering into a treaty that—as matters went—had to be disallowed, with some discredit to the Empire, and some risk of a rupture of its friendly relations with a foreign power.

MR. SCOBLE—Does not the House of Commons afford that machinery?

MR. DUNKIN—The House of Commons knows very little, and cares much less, about our local affairs. (Hear, hear.) I say, if there had then been a Colonial Council at home, where representatives of the different provincial administrations might have met and advised with any of Her Majesty's ministers, there would have been no difficulty. It would have disposed of any number of other questions more satisfactorily than they have been disposed of. The north-eastern boundary question with the States, for instance, would never have been settled in a way so little accordant with our views and interests; and the question of the western boundary would have been settled sooner and better, also. Take another illustration. When the difficulty arose between this country and England about our tariff, when the Sheffield manufacturers sought to create a feeling at home against us, because we, mainly to raise revenue, placed duties higher than they liked on importations of manufactured goods, if any such machinery had been in operation, no such wide-spread and mischievous misapprehension as to our acts and purposes could have arisen, as ever since has been prevalent in England, and even on the floor of the House of Commons. In fact, I repeat that without some such system, I do not see how our relations with the Empire can be maintained on a satisfactory footing. It is just the want of it that is leading so many at home now to think us in a transition state towards separation and independence, when, in truth, we have such need to prove to them that we are in a transition state towards a something very different indeed — the precise antipodes of separation. (Hear, hear.) Sir, I was saying that in this scheme there is no such conservative tendency as this—nothing indicative of a set purpose to develope, strengthen and perpetuate our connection with the Empire. That end we might indeed better gain without than with this extra machinery of local federation; for disguise it how you may, the idea that underlies this plan is this, and nothing else—that we are to create here a something—kingdom, viceroyalty, or principality—something that will soon stand in the same position towards the British Crown that Scotland and Ireland stood in before they were legislatively united with England; a something having no other tie to the Empire than the one tie of fealty to the British Crown—a tie which in the cases, first, of Scotland, and then of Ireland, was found, when the pinch came, to be no tie at all; which did not restrain either Scotland or Ireland from courses so inconsistent with that of England as to have made it necessary that their relations should be radically changed, and a legislative union formed in place of a merely nominal union. Suppose you do create here a kingdom or a principality, bound to the Empire by this shadow of a tie, the day of trial cannot be far distant, when this common fealty will be found of as little use in our case as it was in theirs; when, in consequence, the question will force itself on the Empire and on us between entire separation on the one hand, and a legislative union on the other. But a legislative union of British America with the United Kingdom must be, in the opinion of, one may say, everybody at home and here, a sheer utter impossibility; and when the question shall come to be whether we are so to be merged in the United Kingdom or are to separate entirely from it, the answer can only be—"At whatever cost, we separate." Sir, I believe in my conscience that this step now proposed is one directly and inevitably tending to that other step; and for that reason—even if I believed, as I do not, that it bid fair to answer ever so well in the other respects—because I am an Englishman and hold to the connection with England, I must be against this scheme. Suppose now, on the other hand, this scheme were not to go into operation, there would be no earthly difficulty in working out, with this Canada of ours, the other plan I have been suggesting for the placing of our relations with the Empire on a better footing. Nor would there probably be any material difficulty either in bringing about a legislative union of the Lower Provinces, or in developing a very near approach to free trade, or indeed absolute free trade between us and them. I know there are those who say that this mock Federal union is necessary in order to our getting that free trade with those provinces. Well, sir, as to that, all I care to say is this, that for a number of years past we have had a near approach to free trade with the United States—a foreign country; and I imagine we can have it with the Lower Provinces as well, without any very great difficulty. (Hear, hear.) I say again, we had far better hold firmly to the policy of thus maintaining and strengthening our union with the parent state, than let ourselves, under whatever pretext, be drawn into this other course, which must inevitably lead to our separation from the Empire. (Hear, hear.) But, Mr. SPEAKER, there is still another point of view in which this scheme requires to be considered. The people of the United States, when they framed their institutions, were not only starting as a nation—they were so starting with no dangerous neighbor-nation near them. If we are

to take the step now urged upon us, not only are we to be something less than a nation, but we are to be this with a very dangerous neighbor-nation indeed. In this connection I may be allowed to read a few words. The thirtieth resolution says:—

The General Government and Parliament shall have all powers necessary or proper for performing the obligations of the Federated Provinces, as part of the British Empire, to foreign countries, arising under treaties between Great Britain and such countries.

It is quite right that the General Government should have such powers; but the very fact of our having to make a reservation of this kind, is an unpleasant recognition of the fact, in itself the reverse of encouraging, of the all darkening neighborhood of the United States. It is a most singular thing that we are required on the one hand to go into this union on this very account—for downright dread of the United States—and yet that on the other, we are as confidently assured of our own immense resources, are told that we are so wonderfully great and wonderfully rich, that we are something like—I don't know whether we are not—the third or fourth power, or maritime power, one or other, in the world. Really, I would not undertake to say how great we are, or are not, according to honorable gentlemen. They startle one. I had no idea how great we were! (Hear, hear.) But yet, with all this wonderful magnificence and greatness, we are told we positively must not, for very fear of the United States—for fear of their power—for fear of their hostility, we must not any longer stay disunited, but must instantly enter into this so-called union. Just as if either their power or their hostility towards us—taking that to be their feeling—would be lessened by our doing so. Just as if they would not be only the more jealous of us and hostile to us, for our setting ourselves up ostentatiously as their rivals. (Hear, hear.) In this connection, it does seem to me that we have more than one question to answer. Many honorable gentlemen appear to think they have done all that need be done, when they have answered to their own satisfaction the one question, What is the amount of our resources? Starting with the vastness of our territory, they go into all kinds of statements as to our trade and so forth, multiplying tonnage impossibly, adding together exports and imports—those of the Intercolonial trade and all. I only wonder they do not, on the same principle, calculate our inter-county and our inter-township tradings, or our dealings between cities and country, adding exports and imports of course all round, and so proving that we have done more trade than all the rest of the world put together; unless, indeed, they were to count up the trade of the rest of the world by the same rule;*and then to be sure they would find out that, after all, the rest of the world do more business, are more populous, richer, and stronger, than we. The question is not simply, What are our own resources? We must supplement it with a second—What are they comparatively? And especially, what are they as compared with those of the United States? And while we are asking this question, we may as well not take it for granted as a fact, that the larger our country the stronger we must be. Suppose we are to be four millions of people in a country as large as Europe or larger. I wish to Heaven we were four millions of people—with all the adjacent unexposed territory you will—but in a country smaller than England. Why, sir, New England alone has more population and resources, all told, than the Lower Provinces and Lower Canada together; and with her compactness and advantage of position, she could alone, presumably, beat both.

HON. ATTY. GEN. CARTIER—New England stronger than the Lower Provinces and the two Canadas?

MR. DUNKIN—I did not say that; I said stronger than Lower Canada and the Lower Provinces.

HON. ATTY. GEN. CARTIER—It is about the same in population, two and a half millions, while we have more shipping than they.

MR. DUNKIN—I fear that if we were to come into collision, a good deal of shipping might change hands. At any rate, at the best, we should have a pretty tight time of it. (Hear, hear.)

AN HON. MEMBER—Better put a bold face on it.

MR. DUNKIN—Yes, yes. "Brag is a good dog, but Holdfast is a better." Then, there is the State of New York, which would certainly be more than a match for Upper Canada—and New York is but one of several states conterminous with Upper Canada. Who in his senses, sir, thinks of these provinces as able, of themselves, to hold their own against New England, New York and the rest of the tier of states along our frontier? And yet we are talked to as if Confederation were about to make us the

third or fourth power, or maritime power in the world! But what I was saying more particularly was, that too much of territory, and above all too much of exposed frontier, does not increase our strength, but lessens it. Ours is the 'long thin line of red," which is not so well able to receive a charge as the solid square.

COL. HAULTAIN was understood to signify dissent to some of the propositions here advanced.

MR. DUNKIN—If the hon. member for Peterborough thinks that in a military point of view, the length and narrowness of our territory adds to our strength—if he thinks we are the stronger for our length of frontier, I would respectfully reco mmend him to attend one of our military schools (Laughter.) But seriously, sir, if we are to compare our resources with those of the United States, we shall find, as I have said, that theirs are unmistakably, and beyond count, greater.

COL. HAULTAIN—Than the British Empire?

MR. DUNKIN—That is not the comparison. We are continually hearing of what Confederation is to do for ourselves, how it is going to make us a great power in the world. It is going to do nothing of the kind. But again—and here is a third question that in this connection we have got to answer—how is the temper of the United States going to be affected, on the one hand, by the policy here urged on us, of what I may call hostile independent effort—effort made on our part, with the avowed object of setting ourselves up as a formidable power against them; or on the other hand, by a policy such as I have been urging, of unobtrusive development of our institutions in connection with the British Empire? In which of the two cases are they likely to be the more amiable, or, (which is perhaps more to the point), the less aggressive or practically unamiable, as our neighbors? Besides, there comes up still another question. What is to be the attitude of Great Britain under either of these two suppositions? As I have said, the question is, first, as to our own resources; next, as to the comparative resources of the United States; then, as to their attitude and temper towards us, upon one or other of these two suppositions; then, as to the attitude and temper of Great Britain, in reference to each of these suppositions; and lastly, as to the re action (so to speak) upon ourselves, of these respective attitudes of the two countries in either case.

If, sir, we are thinking to give other people the idea, that by uniting ourselves together in any such way as this, we are going to make ourselves able to take care of ourselves, we are merely humbugging ourselves, and trying to humbug others. The people of the United States are stronger than we are, and are known so to be; and if we are to hold our own against or beside them, it can only be by remaining strongly, avowedly, lastingly, attached to Great Britain. This is the firm conclusion I have come to; and I believe it is the conclusion to which any one who will give his thoughtful attention to the subject must come also. And I must and do protest against the notion which seems to prevail among the advocates of this scheme, that somehow or other it is going so to increase our power, as to make us a formidable neighbor of the United States. The danger is, of its making that people more jealous of us and more hostile towards us than before. And if, besides that, it is going to give them and the people of England, or either of them, the idea that as a result of it we are to care less for the connection with the Empire than before—that under it we are before long to go alone, it is going to commit us to about the saddest fatal mistake that a people ever made. (Hear, hear.) Mr. SPEAKER, I must apologize for the length to which I have wearied the House. (Cries of "Go on!") I have gone through, as well as I could, the leading points of my arguments, so far; and have indicated a number of points of contrast between this system and that of the United States. I trust I have not been too prolix in my attempts to shew that the Constitution now offered for our acceptance presents machinery entirely unlike that of the United States, and entirely unlike that of the British Empire—that it is inconsistent with either—that so far from its proffering to us all the advantages of both and the disadvantages of neither, it rather presents to us the disadvantages of both and the advantages of neither; that so far from its tending to improve our relations either with the Mother Country or with the United States, it holds out to us very little prospect indeed for the future, in either of these respects. (Hear, hear.) I shall not attempt to review my argument on these heads, for I do not think that to anyone at all willing to reflect, what I have advanced can require to be proved more fully. If I am not entirely wrong, the only

way in which this proposed machinery can be got to work at all, will be by an aggregation, so to speak, in the first Federal Cabinet, of the leading men of the different existing provincial administrations. The attempt must be made to combine the six majorities, so as to carry on an administration in harmony with the understood wishes of the six several provinces, irrespectively of every consideration of principle, or of sound far-seeing policy. I do not see how, although this thing may be done at starting, it can be carried on—I was going to say, for any length of time—I might say, for any time, long or short, unless by a system of the most enormous jobbery and corruption. Whenever any sore spot shall show itself—and we may rely on it, there will be more than one such show itself very soon—then feuds and divisions of the worst sort will follow, and the machinery will no longer work. Unfortunately, there are in it none of those facilities for harmonious workings, none of those nice adaptations by which the stronger power is so tempered as not to fall too harshly on the weaker. Just so long as the majorities in all the different provinces work cordially together, well and good. But they cannot possibly work harmoniously together long; and so soon as they come into collision, there comes trouble, and with the trouble, the fabric is at an end. (Hear, hear.) For myself, I am decidedly of opinion that our true interest is to hold this machinery over, to consider it carefully, to see if something better cannot be devised. (Hear, hear.) I am sure there can. But instead of that, we are called upon emphatically and earnestly at once to throw aside all considerations to the contrary, and to adopt the measure; and we are at the same time told, in unmistakable language, that we positively cannot—must not—shall not—change a single word of it. Various considerations are urged upon us for this unseemly haste; considerations connected with the attitude of the United States, with Great Britain, with the Lower Provinces, and with our own domestic affairs. With the permission of the House, I will touch as briefly as I can on these four classes of considerations, and then cease longer to weary the House. I begin, then, with the considerations connected with the attitude of the United States, which are urged upon us as reasons why we should rush into this measure of Confederation. To some extent I have already incidentally touched on these in another connexion; but they call for some further notice, and in giving it them, I will try not to repeat myself. Judging from much of the language which we have heard on the floor of this House, one would suppose we must be on the verge of a war with the United States. For my part, I believe nothing of the kind. But if we were, would it be at all the right thing for us to abstain from the more pressing questions of our defences and the organization of the militia, and to be instead discussing here these plans of a Federal Union, Provincial Constitutions, and I know not what? These we are called upon, I admit, to discuss in a tremendous hurry, to settle off-hand, in workable or unworkable shape, nobody seeming to know or to care which, everybody professing to hope that all will come right in the end, whether he thinks it will or not. But, sir, I say again, if war were imminent with the United States, the one question for us would be the state of our defences, the organization of our militia, how much England can do for us, how much we can do for ourselves, how much England and we, each of us, are to undertake to do together. That is not the question at the present time at all, and I therefore take it that the outcry raised in connection with this scheme, about our defences and the militia, is just so much buncombe. (Hear, hear.) If honorable gentlemen opposite believed in it, I am certain that the pressing question would be taken up first. Further, if such danger were not even pretty far off, I for one would be disposed to think that the taking up now of this other class of questions comes a little late in the day. With any near, real danger of war with the United States, it would be quite too late for us to be sitting here, gravely discussing a political union, to be consummated months hence, at soonest, and then only to lead to the construction of railways which will take years, and defences which cannot be put in order for months or years, and to future developments of all kinds, which it will take years on years to carry out. If war, I say, is imminent, these ulterior undertakings, though begun now, would be begun all too late. Whenever there is such danger, our defence will not be found in the making of federal or other constitutions, or in paper display of any kind, but must be found in the strong arms and determined courage of our people, responding earnestly to the call of the Mother Country, and backed with all the power she can bring to bear upon the conflict. Supposing that time come, we have plenty of governing machinery for that defence. We do not need, in order to it, a viceroy and court, and lieutenant-governors, and all the complicated political apparatus of this scheme. We could get along just as well under our present system, and I think better. Certainly, if modified as I have indicated it might be—if improved by the better development of our relations to the Empire—the system which would thence result would be as good as that here offered for our acceptance—indeed, would be much better. But, sir, the real danger is not of war with the United States. It is from what I may call their pacific hostility—from trouble to be wrought by them within this country—trouble to arise out of refusal of reciprocity—repeal of the bonding system—custom-house annoyances—passport annoyances; from their fomenting difficulties here, and taking advantage of our local jealousies; from the multiplied worries they may cause us by a judicious alternation of bullying and coaxing, the thousand incidents which may easily be made to happen if things are not going on quite well in this country, and the people and government of the States are minded to make us feel the consequences of our not getting on quite so well as we might. Whether the union of the States is restored or not, this kind of thing can go on. The danger is, that either the whole United States, or those portions of the United States which are near us, and which are really stronger than we are, and enterprising enough and ambitious enough, and not very fond of us, and not at all fond of the Mother Country, not at all unwilling to strike a blow at her and to make us subservient to their own interest and ambition—the danger is, I say, that the United States, or those portions of the United States near us, may avail themselves of every opportunity to perplex us, to embroil us in trouble, to make us come within the disturbing influences of their strong local attraction.—Now, to pretend to tell me that the United States or the Northern States, whichever you please, are going to be frightened, from a policy of that kind, by our taking upon ourselves great airs, and forming ourselves into a grand Confederation, is to tell me that their people are, like the Chinese, a people to be frightened by loud noises and ugly grimaces. (Laughter.) I do not believe they are. They are not to be frightened by any union we can make here. They have among them politicians, to say the least, quite as bold, shrewd and astute as any we have here. The danger will just be that of our having agitation of our own going on here, and internal troubles, while these annoyances on the part of our neighbors across the border are being multiplied upon us; and that England may at the same time be feeling that the tie between her and us is more or less relaxed, and that wrong and humiliation put upon us do not concern her so much as they would have done when our connection with her was practically more intimate. In and before 1840, after the troubles which had been distracting Canada were put down, it was declared, and perfectly well understood, that the Imperial Government was simply determined to hold on to the connection with this country. And the knowledge of that expressed determination guaranteed us a pretty long term of comparative freedom from annoyances and trouble of the kind to which I have been referring. If, now, a different idea is to prevail—if the notion is to go abroad that we are, by creating ourselves into a new nationality, to be somewhat less connected with the Empire than these provinces heretofore have been, then I do apprehend that a very different future is before us, and that in all sorts of ways, by vexations of all kinds, by the fomenting of every trouble within our own borders, whether originating from abroad, or only reacted on from abroad, we shall be exposed to dangers of the most serious kind. And, therefore, so far from seeing in our relations towards the United States, any reason why we should assume a position of semi-independence, an attitude of seeming defiance towards them, I find in them the strongest reason why, even while regarding, or affecting to regard them as little as possible, we should endeavor to make all the world see that we are trying to strengthen our union with the Mother Country—that we care far less about a mere union with neighboring provinces, which will frighten no one in the least, but that we are determined to maintain at all hazards and draw closer, that connection with the Mother Country which alone, so long as it lasts, can and will protect us from all serious aggression. (Hear, hear.) But we are told that, on account of a variety of considerations connected with the state of opinion at home, and out of deference to that opinion, we must positively carry out this scheme. Well, there are two or three questions to be answered here. What is that

opinion at home? What is it worth? And what sort of lesson does it teach us? There are some distinctions which, in my judgment, must be drawn with reference to this. There are different phases of opinion prevailing at home, which must be taken into account. I have great respect for some home opinions. Many things they know in England much better than we do. Some things they do not know so well. They do not know so much about ourselves as we do; and they do not occupy their minds so much with that class of questions which relate merely to our interests, as we at any rate ought to do; and on these matters I am not sure that we shall act wisely if we yield at once to the first expressions of opinion at home. But now, sir, what is the opinion at home, or rather, what are the opinions entertained at home, with reference to this measure? Of course, I do not intend to weary the House with a long detailed statement on this subject. But I must say this—and I do not think that any one who knows anything at all about it will contradict what I state—there is at home a considerably numerous, and much more loud-speaking than numerous, class of politicians who do not hesitate to say that it is not for the interest of England to keep her colonies at all.

Mr. SCOBLE—Not numerous.

Mr. DUNKIN—Well, I think they are rather numerous and pretty influential, and they make a good deal of stir; and some of them being in pretty high places, there is danger that their views may exercise a good deal of influence upon public opinion at home. There are many influences at work at home, tending to the prevalence of the idea that the sooner the colonies leave the Mother Country, the better—and especially that the sooner these colonies leave the Mother Country, the better. There is a very exaggerated notion at home of danger to the peace of the Empire from the maintenance of British supremacy in this part of the world. That is the fact; and there is no use in our shutting our eyes to it. We may just as well take it, uncomfortable and hard fact as it may be. If we choose to tell ourselves it is not the fact, we are only humbugging ourselves. (Hear, hear.) That is one point, as regards public opinion in England. Another is, as to the appreciation, at home, of this particular scheme. I take it, that what we are told on this head by those who urge this scheme upon us, about opinion at home, amounts to this —that at home this scheme is regarded with very great favor, that we are expected to adopt it, and that if we do not adopt it, it will be the better for us with reference to home public opinion. Well, the questions for us are : What is the opinion at home about this scheme ? What is the opinion entertained in high quarters as to its goodness or badness ; and if there is an opinion in favor of the scheme being adopted, from what considerations does that opinion, to a great extent, prevail ? I am not going into these questions minutely, but I must be allowed to make a remark or two as to the opinion expressed by Her Majesty's Government with regard to this scheme. I have already, to some extent, alluded to the dispatch of the Colonial Secretary ; but in this connection, I must allude to it a little further. (Hear, hear.) It is clear from that dispatch that the Colonial Secretary wrote under these impressions : first of all, he was under the idea that this scheme had been drawn up by the representatives of every province, chosen by the respective governors, without distinction of party. That was not quite the case. There were representatives from the two leading parties in each of the other provinces, but it was not so as regarded Lower Canada. (Hear, hear.) The Colonial Secretary was, besides, evidently under the impression that when these gentlemen came together, they gave the matters before them the most mature deliberation. He says :—" They have conducted their deliberations with patient sagacity, and have arrived at unanimous conclusions on questions involving many difficulties." The " patient sagacity " was exercised for seventeen or nineteen days, and the " unanimous conclusions " were, after all, certainly not unanimous. The Secretary goes on to say :—

Her Majesty's Government have given to your despatch and to the resolutions of the Conference, their most deliberate consideration. They have regarded them as a whole, and as having been designed by those who framed them, to establish as complete and perfect a union of the whole, into one government, as the circumstances of the case, and a due consideration of existing interests, would admit. They accept them, therefore, as being in the deliberate judgment of those best qualified to decide upon the subject, the best framework of a measure to be passed by the Imperial Parliament for attaining that most desirable result.

Her Majesty's Government thus take for granted a " deliberate " examination, which most unquestionably never has been given to this crude project. Now, with all this, with the impression that men of all parties had here acted in combination, when in truth they have done no such thing ; that patient sagacity had been expended on the framing of the scheme, when in truth there was nothing of the kind ; that the conclusions were unanimously arrived at, which again was not the fact ; with all this, Her Majesty's Government have only come to the point of giving a very general, and, as any one who reads the dispatch can see, a very qualified approval of the scheme. First, an objection is raised as to the want of accurate determination' of the limits between the authority of the Central and that of the local legislatures. I will not read the words, as I read them last night, but no one can read the dispatch without seeing that the language of the Colonial Secretary on that point is the language of diplomatic disapproval (Hear, hear.) Though he gives a general approval, he criticises and evidently does not approve. He sees an intention, but calls attention to the fact that that intention is not clearly and explicitly expressed. He then goes on and makes another objection—the financial. His language is this :—

Her Majesty's Government cannot but express the earnest hope, that the arrangements which may be adopted in this respect may not be of such a nature as to increase—at least in any considerable degree—the whole expenditure, or to make any material addition to the taxation, and thereby retard the internal industry, or tend to impose new burdens on the commerce of the country.

The hope that it will not be is the diplomatic way of hinting a fear that it may be. When Her Majesty's Government is driven to " hope" that these arrangements will not increase in any considerable degree the whole expenditure, or make any material addition to taxation, and thereby retard internal industry, or tend to impose new burdens on the commerce of the country, it is perfectly clear that they see that in the scheme which makes them tolerably sure it will. And then we have a third objection :—

Her Majesty's Government are anxious to lose no time in conveying to you their general approval of the proceedings of the Conference. There are, however, two provisions of great importance which seem to require revision. The first of these is the provision contained in the 44th resolution, with respect to the exercise of the prerogative of pardon.

That is emphatically declared to be entirely

wrong. And then comes the fourth objection : "The second point which Her Majesty's Government desire should be reconsidered"—and this phrase is positively, so far as words can give it, a command on the part of Her Majesty's Government that it shall be reconsidered :—

The second point which Her Majesty's Government desire should be reconsidered is the constitution of the Legislative Council. They appreciate the considerations which have influenced the Conference in determining the mode in which this body, so important to the constitution of the Legislature, should be composed. But it appears to them to require further consideration whether, if the members be appointed for life, and their number be fixed, there will be any sufficient means of restoring harmony between the Legislative Council and the popular Assembly, if it shall ever unfortunately happen that a decided difference of opinion shall arise between them. These two points, relating to the prerogative of the Crown and the Constitution of the Upper Chamber have appeared to require distinct and separate notice.

Is not that a pretty emphatic dissent?

Questions of minor consequence and matters of detailed arrangement may properly be reserved for a future time, when the provisions of the bill intended to be submitted to the Imperial Parliament shall come under consideration.

So, sir, there are more objections still which the Colonial Secretary has not stated. He gives a general sanction, but specifies four matters, two of which he distinctly says must be altered, and the other two he does not approve of, and he says that other matters—too numerous, I suppose, to specify—must be reserved for remark at a future time. Well, just at the time that this despatch made its appearance, there was an article in the London *Times*, a passage from which I will read in this connection, though it may seem to bear on a somewhat different branch of the question from that with which I am just more particularly dealing. The London *Times*, referring to this despatch, makes use of these expressions, and I beg the attention of the House to them, because they give the key-note of a great deal of the public opinion at home with reference to this matter :—

It is true we are not actually giving up the American colonies,—nay, the despatch we are quoting does not contain the slightest hint that such a possibility ever crossed the mind of the writer; but yet it is perfectly evident—and there is no use in concealing the fact—that the Confederation movement considerably diminishes the difficulty which would be felt by the colonies in separating from the Mother Country. Even now the North American Confederation represents a state formidable from the numbers of its hardy and energetic population, and capable, if so united, of vigorously defending the territories it possesses. A few years will add greatly to that population, and place Canada, Hochelaga, Acadia, or by whatever other name the Confederacy may think fit to call itself, quite out of the reach of invasion or conquest. Such a state would not only be strong against the Mother Country under the impossible supposition of our seeking to coerce it by force, but it might be separated from us without incurring the disgrace of leaving a small and helpless community at the mercy of powerful and warlike neighbors.

Here, then, is the somewhat less diplomatic utterance of the *Times*, on the occasion of the appearance of this despatch. It is perfectly true that no hint was given officially, when this scheme was sent home, that it contemplated separation. Perfectly true, that in the answer there is no hint that separation is contemplated. But it is perfectly true, also, that the leading journal instantly sees in it, and seizes at, the possibility—first, of its greatly facilitating our going—and, secondly, of its greatly facilitating, on the part of the Mother Country, the letting of us go. I shall come back to this branch of the subject presently, after I shall have quoted from a much more important expression of public opinion than any article in the *Times*. Meantime, I must refer to the language of Her Majesty's Speech from the Throne. It has been read during this debate already, and has been read as if it contained the most emphatic approval possible of this whole scheme—so emphatic an approval, that even to assume to discuss it now would seem to amount almost to treason. This language, of course, it is needless to say, is that of Her Majesty's Imperial advisers, and is to be read in connection with what Her Majesty's Government have said about this plan in the Colonial Secretary's despatch—that before it is passed into an enactment, it will require a good deal of revision. We may be told here that the document before us is a treaty, on which not a line or letter of amendment can be made by us. But Her Majesty's Government clearly understand that they are not bound by it, and that they are to alter it as much as they please. They won't give the pardoning power to these lieutenant-governors; they won't constitute the Legislative Council in this way; they won't look with indifference to the incurring of unheard-of expenses, and the hampering of commerce which they consider to be implied in this scheme. No, they are to look into this thing, to look into the details of what they evidently think to be a pretty crude scheme; while we, who are most interested, are required by our local rulers not to look into it at all, but just to accept it at their hands as a whole. The language addressed from the Throne to the Imperial Parliament is this: "Her Majesty has had great satisfaction in giving Her sanction"—to what? —"to the meeting of a conference of delegates from the several North American Provinces, who, on invitation from Her Majesty's Governor General, assembled at Quebec." Certainly; we knew that before; they assembled without Her Majesty's sanction, but they got her sanction afterwards to their having so assembled. "These delegates adopted resolutions having for their object a closer union of those provinces under a central government. If those resolutions shall be approved by the provincial legislatures, a bill will be laid before you for carrying this important measure into effect" —not for giving full effect to the details of this scheme, but for carrying the measure— the closer union—in the shape the Imperial Government may give it, into effect. That is all. (Hear, hear.) Take this along with the despatch of the Colonial Secretary. If it is a declaration that this thing is a treaty, which may not be amended by us without flying in the face of Her Majesty's Government, I do not understand the meaning of words. (Hear, hear.) In connection with the Speech from the Throne, we had, the other night, some notice taken, on the floor of this House, of language used in discussing the address in the Imperial Parliament. Lords CLAREMONT, HOUGHTON, GRANVILLE and DERBY had something to say in respect of this scheme in the House of Lords; as also, Mr. HANBURY TRACY in the House of Commons. I do not attach great weight to what was there said, because there really was little said any way, and that little could not indicate any great amount of knowledge upon the subject treated. However, I will quote first what the mover of the address, the Earl of CLAREMONT, said. After referring to the war in New Zealand, he went on :—

My Lords, although these operations in India, New Zealand, and Japan, are matters of more or less interest or concern to the nation, and, as such, are fully deserving of notice, yet they are small in comparison to the importance of the probable change in the constitution of our North American Colonies. Since the declaration of independence by the colonies, since known as the United States of America, so great a scheme of self-government, or one shadowing forth so many similar and possible changes, has not occurred.

Now, I cannot read this sentence without asking what analogy there is between this project and the declaration of independence. Why should these resolutions suggest to any one's mind the declaration of independence? Did the gentlemen who signed these resolutions in order to authenticate them—pledge their lives and fortunes, and I don't know what besides, to anything, or risk anything, by appending their signatures to the document? Was it a great exercise of political heroism? Why, the men who signed the declaration of independence qualified themselves in the eyes of the Imperial Government for the pleasant operations of heading and hanging. They knew what they were about. They were issuing a rebel declaration of war. But this is a piece of machinery, on the face of it at least, to perpetuate our connection with the Mother Country! Why then does it suggest the idea that so great a scheme of self-government, or one shadowing forth so many similar and possible changes, "hardly ever before occurred?" It is because there is, underlying the speaker's thought, just that idea of the anti-colonial school in England, that we are going to slip away from our connection with the Mother Country; and in this respect, therefore, it seems to him that it is like the declaration of independence. The remaining sentence indicates a curious misapprehension as to the present posture of this question. "If the delegates of these several colonies finally agree to the resolutions framed by their committee, and if these resolutions be approved by the several legislatures of the several colonies, Parliament will be asked to consider and complete this federation of our Northern American possessions." The noble lord, the mover of the Address, seems to take the resolutions for a mere report of a committee which (on their way here) had yet to be submitted to the consideration of the delegates! Next, I turn to the language of Lord HOUGHTON, the seconder of the Address; and from his lips too, we have an almost distinct utterance of the idea of our coming independence. He says :—

That impulse which inclines small states to bind themselves together for the purpose of mutual protection and for the dignity of empire, has shewn itself in two remarkable examples, of which I may be permitted to say a few words. In Europe it has manifested itself in the case of Italy, which is not, indeed, alluded to in any part of Her Majesty's speech, because it is an accomplished fact of European history. A convention has lately taken place between the Emperor of the French and the King of Italy, in which England can take no other interest than to hope that it may redound to the prosperity of the one and the honor of the other. At any rate, one great advantage has been accomplished. With his capital in the centre of Italy it is no longer possible to talk of Victor Emmanuel as King of Piedmont. He is King of Italy, or nothing. On the other side of the Atlantic the same impulse—[that same impulse, which, in the case of Italy, the speaker characterizes as aiming at the dignity of empire]—the same impulse had manifested itself in the proposed amalgamation of the northern provinces of British America. I heartily concur in all—[the all being as we have just seen, not much]—that has been said by my noble friend the mover of this address in his laudation of that project. It is, my lords, a most interesting contemplation that that project has arisen, and has been approved by Her Majesty's Government. It is certainly contrary to what might be considered the old maxims of government in connection with the colonies, that we should here express —and that the Crown itself should express— satisfaction at a measure which tends to bind together, in almost independent power, our colonies in North America. We do still believe that though thus banded together, they will recognize the value of British connection, and that while they will be safer in this amalgamation, we shall be as safe in their fealty. The measure will no doubt, my lords, require much prudent consideration and great attention to provincial susceptibilities.

I repeat, Mr. SPEAKER, there is in this quotation a second pretty-plainly-expressed anticipation of our nearly approaching independence. We are supposed, by one of these noble lords, to be taking a step analogous to that taken by the authors of the Declaration of Independence; and by the other, to be moved by the same impulse of empire that has been leading to the establishment of the Kingdom of Italy.

MR. SCOBLE—It is a case of want of information.

MR. DUNKIN—Yes, I have no doubt it is a case of want of correct information, and not the only one of its kind. And now, sir, for Lord DERBY's remarks, which also have been quoted here. Certainly, they are in a different, and to my mind a more satisfactory, tone; but they are suggestive, for all that, of an idea that is unwelcome. After remarking on certain passages indicative, in his view, of unfriendly feeling on the part of the United States towards Great Britain and towards us—their threatened abrogation of the reciprocity treaty, arming on the lakes, and so forth—Lord DERBY says :—

Under these circumstances I see with additional satisfaction—[Meaning of, course, though courtesy may have disallowed the phrase, "less dissatisfaction," for he certainly did not see those other matters with any satisfaction at all]— I see with additional satisfaction the announcement of a contemplated important step. I mean the proposed Federation of the British American Provinces. (Hear, hear.) I hope I may regard that Federation as a measure tending to constitute a power strong enough, with the aid of this country, which I trust may never be withdrawn from those provinces, to acquire an importance which, separately, they cou'd not obtain. (Hear, hear.) If I saw in this Federation a desire to separate from this country, I should think it a matter of much more doubtful policy and advantage ; but I perceive with satisfaction, that no such wish is entertained. Perhaps it is premature to discuss, at present, resolutions not yet submitted to the different provincial legislatures, but I hope I see in the terms of that Federation an earnest desire on the part of the provinces to maintain for themselves the blessing of the connection with this country, and a determined and deliberate preference for monarchical over republican institutions.

(Hear, hear.) Now, what I have to say is this, that while I think no man ought to find fault with any of the sentiments here uttered, they are yet the utterances of a statesman who betrays in those utterances at least, as they sound to me, a certain amount of scarcely-concealed apprehension. When a man in the position of Lord DERBY, master of the whole art of expression, speaks at once so hypothetically and so guardedly, falls back upon " I hope I may regard," " I trust may never be," " I hope I see," and so forth, one feels that there is an under-current of thought, not half concealed by such expressions, to the effect that there is too much danger of the very things so hoped and trusted against coming to pass at no very distant period.

HON. ATTY. GEN. CARTIER—I see the reverse of that. (Hear, hear.)

MR. DUNKIN—Well, the hon. gentleman sees differently from what I do. If there had been no doubt whatever in the mind of Lord DERBY, as to our want of strength, the growth of the anti-colonial party at home, and the tendency of this sche e towards separation, his hope and trust to the contrary, would either have been unuttered, or would have been uttered in another tone. I am well enough satisfied that Lord DERBY himself has not the most remote idea of falling in with the views of the so-called colonial reformers in England, who desire to see the colonies pay for every thing or be cast off; but he knows the hold that their views have gained at home, and he speaks accordingly. And there is no doubt, sir, that this feeling has been got up in England to an extent very much to be regretted. In this connection I have yet to notice some passages—and I shall deal with them as briefly as I can—from the very important article I quoted last night, which is contained in the *Edinburgh Review* for January, and which, I am sorry to say, expresses this feeling in the strongest possible form. But before citing them, I am bound to say that I by no means believe the views they express are universally or even generally entertained at home. I do believe, though, that they are entertained by many, and that there is much danger of their doing a vast deal of mischief. That they are loudly avowed, does not admit of doubt; and when we find them set forth in the pages of so influential an organ of opinion as the *Edinburgh Review*, the case assumes a very serious aspect. There are other passages in the article to the same effect as those I am about to read, and which might, perhaps, be quoted with advantage, did time allow. Well, here is one occurring early in the article :—

There are problems of colonial policy the solution of which cannot, without peril, be indefinitely delayed; and though Imperial England is doing her best to keep up appearances in the management of her five and forty dependencies, the political links which once bound them to each other and to their common centre are evidently worn out. Misgivings haunt the public mind as to the stability of an edifice which seems to be founded on a reciprocity of deception, and only to be shored up for the time by obsolete and meaningless traditions.

When an utterance like this finds its way into the pages of the *Edinburgh Review*, a review which more than almost any other may be held to speak in the name of a large class of the ablest statesmen of England, we have reason to ask what it is all tending to. I never in my life felt more pain in reading anything political, than I felt in reading this article; and I never discharged a more painful duty than I am endeavoring to dis-

8

charge at this moment, in commenting on it. But truth is truth, and must be told. A little farther on, the same writer proceeds :—

It is not unnatural that the desire to maintain a connection with the power and wealth of the Mother Country should be stronger on the side of the colonies than it is on that of the British public, for they owe almost everything to us, and we receive but little from them. Moreover, the existing system of colonial government enables them to combine all the advantages of local independence with the strength and dignity of a great empire. But the Imperial Government in the meantime has to decide, not as of old, whether Great Britain is to tax the colonies, but to what extent the colonies are to be permitted to tax Great Britain—a question which is daily becoming more urgent and less easy of solution.

Further on, the writer goes on to say :—

It might puzzle the wisest of our statesmen, if he were challenged to put his finger on any single item of material advantage resulting to ourselves from our dominions in British North America, which cost us at this moment about a million sterling a year.

They do no such thing; but that is neither here nor there. Then follow these sentences, more galling still :—

Retainers who will neither give nor accept notice to quit our service, must, it is assumed, be kept for our service. There are, nevertheless, special and exceptional difficulties which beset us in this portion of our vast field of empire.

Nearly a page follows of description of what these difficulties are, being mainly those arising out of apprehended dangers from the United States, and thereon is based this observation :—

It is scarcely surprising that any project which may offer a prospect of escape from a political situation so undignified and unsatisfactory should be hailed with a cordial welcome by all parties concerned.

But one meaning can be put upon all this. In the opinion of the writer, England does not believe that these provinces are worth anything to her, while the connection with the Mother Country is worth all to us; and she would hail with satisfaction any way of escape from the obligations and dangers that we are said to cast upon her. I go on a little further, and I find what are his views as to the undertakings that, in connection with this project, we are expected to assume. What I am next quoting forms a foot note; but a foot note is often, like a lady's postscript, more important than the text of the letter :—

A very important question, on which these papers afford no information, is that relating to the future condition of those territories and dependencies of the Crown in North America, which are not included within the present boundaries of the five provinces. We allude more particularly to the territories now held by the Hudson's Bay Company, under the Crown, by charter or lease. The Crown is doubtless bound to take care that the interest of its grantees—[it never seems to have occurred to our friend that we, too, are grantees]—are not prejudiced by these changes; but, on the other hand, an English trading company is ill qualified to carry on the government and provide for the defence of a vast and inaccessible expanse of continental territory.

One would think so, seeing that it is just this territory which this writer has been telling us England shrinks herself from defending :—

Probably, the best and most equitable solution would be the cession of the whole region to the Northern Federation for a fair indemnity—[probably enough, from a point of view not ours—(hear, hear)]—and this would lead to the execution of the Great Northern Pacific Railway, under the auspices of the Federal power.

Would it? (Hear, hear, and laughter.)
Hon. Atty. Gen. CARTIER—Hear! hear!
Hon. Mr. HOLTON—Is that the policy?
Hon. Atty. Gen. CARTIER—Hear! hear!
Mr. DUNKIN—A little further on, in the article, I find some amplification of this grand programme :—

The result of these proposals, if carried into effect, would be the creation of a new state in North America, still retaining the name of a British dependency, comprising an area about equal to that of Europe, a population of about four millions, with an aggregate revenue in sterling of about two millions and a half, and carrying on a trade (including exports, imports and intercolonial commerce) of about twenty-eight millions sterling per annum. If we consider the relative positions of Canada and the Maritime Provinces—the former possessing good harbors, but no back country, the former an unlimited supply of cereals, but few minerals; the latter an unlimited supply of iron and coal, but little agricultural produce. The commercial advantages of union between states so circumstanced, are too obvious to need comment. The completion of the Intercolonial Railway, and the probable annexation of the fertile portions of the North-Western territory to the new Confederation,

form a portion only of the probable consequences of its formation, but in which Europe and the world at large will eventually participate. When the ——

Hon. Mr. McDOUGALL — The hon. gentleman should do justice to the reviewer. He leaves out an important passage.
Mr. DUNKIN—What is it?
Hon. Mr. McDOUGALL—After the word "formation," the following words are given :—"The benefits of which will not be limited to the colonies alone, but," &c. Taken with the context, these words are important.
Hon. Mr. McGEE—Hear! hear!
Mr. DUNKIN—An ironical cheer is an easy thing to raise; but I fancy my character hardly warrants the insinuation that I would dishonestly falsify a quotation. I wrote out these extracts hurriedly, the one procurable copy of the *Review* being sent for while I was writing, and I had no opportunity of comparing my manuscript. I am sorry if in my haste I omitted a single word. [After comparing the passage in the *Review* with his manuscript, the hon. member said]: I find I have omitted exactly one line—certainly by the merest accident; indeed, if any one can suppose I did it on purpose, he must take me for a confounded fool. (Hear, hear.) But to continue my quotation, reading again that last sentence, with its dropped line :—

The completion of the Intercolonial Railway, and the probable annexation of the fertile portions of the Great North-Western territory to the new Confederation, form a portion only of the probable consequences of its formation, the benefits of which will not be limited to the colonies alone, but in which Europe and the world at large will eventually participate. When the Valley of the Saskatchewan shall have been colonized, the communications between the Red River Settlement and Lake Superior completed, and the harbour of Halifax united by one continuous line of railway, with the shores of Lake Huron, the three missing links between the Atlantic and Pacific ocean will have been supplied.

Three pretty large links, by the way, and it would have been more correct if the writer had said "three out of four"—the trifle of the Rocky Mountains being still left for a fourth. (Hear, hear.)
Hon. Mr. McDOUGALL—That is very good.
Mr. DUNKIN—I don't think so; it's rather too good. I have read these portions

of the article to show what we are expected
ly this writer to do. We are to buy the
Hudson's Bay territory, and take care of it,
and make a grand road all across the continent, which Great Britain shrinks from
contemplating herself. And now I will
read just two passages to show how little
sanguine he is of any good to be done by
the scheme as regards ourselves, and in the
conduct of our own affairs. Here is one of
them :—

What we have to fear, and if possible to guard
against. is the constant peril of a three-fold conflict of authority implied in the very existence of
a federation of dependencies retaining, as now
proposed, any considerable share of intercolonial
independence.

Rather a suggestive hint, and which, further
on, is expanded and emphasized thus :—

If, as has been alleged, a legislative union is
unattainable, because inconsistent with due secu-
rities for the rights guaranteed to the French
Canadians, by treaty or by the Quebec Act, and
Federation is therefore the only alternative, the
vital question for the framers of this Constitution
is how the inherent weakness of all federations
can in this instance be cured, and the Central
Government armed with a sovereignty which may
be worthy of the name. It is the essence of all
good governments to have somewhere a true
sovereign power. A sovereignty which ever
eludes your grasp, which has no local habitation,
provincial or imperial, is in fact no government
at all. Sooner or later the shadow of authority
which is reflected from an unsubstantial political
idea must cease to have power among men. It
has been assumed by those who take a sanguine
view of this political experiment, that its authors
have steered clear of the rock on which the
WASHINGTON Confederacy has split. But if the
weakness of the Central Government is the rock
alluded to, we fear that unless in clear water and
smooth seas, the pilot who is to steer this new
craft will need a more perfect chart than the
resolutions of the Quebec Conference afford, to
secure him against the risks of navigation.

So far, then, according to the writer of this
article, we have three points settled. He
considers, and those for whom he writes and
speaks consider, and the *Edinburgh Review*
makes known that it considers—first, that the
retention of these colonies is so manifestly dis-
advantageous to the parent state, that it would
puzzle any statesman to find any reason for
keeping us; next, that a result of this measure is to be the early carrying through by
us of undertakings too vast now for England
not to shrink from; and thirdly, that the
measure itself, viewed as a machinery of

government for ourselves, is not going to
work well. There is still a fourth point.
The measure embodies a proffer of fealty to
the British Crown—and with no hint but
that such fealty, and the correlative duty of
protection, are meant both of them to be
perpetual. How does our writer treat of
this ? He says :—

If the Quebec project were to be regarded as in
any sense a final arrangement, and the equivalent
in honor or power to be derived by the Crown
from the acceptance of so perilous an authority,
were to be weighed in the balance with the
commensurate risks, the safety and dignity of the
proffered position might be very questionable ;
but it is impossible to regard this proposed Federation in any other light than that of a transition
stage to eventual independence ; and in this view
the precise form which Imperial sovereignty may
for the time being assume, becomes a matter of
comparatively secondary importance.

And, as if this was not warning plain enough,
the article closes thus :—

The people of England have no desire to snap
asunder abruptly the slender links which still
unite them with their trans-Atlantic fellow-sub-
jects, or to shorten by a single hour the duration
of their common citizenship. * * *
We are led irresistibly to the inference that this
stage has been well nigh reached in the history
of our trans-Atlantic provinces. Hence it comes
to pass that we accept, not with fear and trem-
bling, but with unmixed joy and satisfaction, a
voluntary proclamation, which, though couched
in the accents of loyalty, and proffering an endur-
ing allegiance to our Queen, falls yet more welcome on our ears as the harbinger of the future
and complete independence of British North
America.

(Hear, hear.) Well, Mr. SPEAKER, I can
only say that if these are the opinions
which honorable gentlemen opposite are
disposed to "hear, hear" approvingly, they
are not mine. I find in them an unmistakable proof that there is an important
party at home who take up this measure,
and hope to see it carried through with the
mere view to its being a step to absolute
independence on our part, and a cutting of
the tie between these provinces and the
parent state. (Hear, hear.) Sir, I look upon
the early cutting of that tie as a certain
result of this measure; and of that again, I
hold the inevitable result to be our early
absorption into the republic south of us—the
United States, or the Northern States, be
which it may. (Hear, hear.) It cannot be,
that we can form here an independent state
that shall have a prosperous history. I say

a..ain, I am far from believing that this idea of separation is by any means the dominant opinior. at home; but I am sure it is entertained by a prominent school of English politicians. (Cries of "Name, name.") It is easy to call for names; but there are too many; one can't go over the names of a whole school. I indicate them well enough when I give them the well-known name of the GOLDWIN-SMITH school. There are influential men enough, and too many, among them — (Renewed cries of "Name") Well then, I rather think Mr. COBDEN, Mr. BRIGHT, and any number more of the Liberal party, belong to this school—in fact, most of what are known as the Manchester school. But, joking apart, if honorable gentlemen in their simplicity believe that utterances of the kind I have been reading appear in the *Edinburgh Review* without significance, their simplicity passes mine. I read these utterances, in connection with those of the *Times* and of any quantity of other English journals, as representing the views of an influential portion of the British public, views which have such weight with the Imperial Government as may go some way to account for the acceptance—the qualified acceptance—which this scheme has met with at their hands. It is recommended at home—strongly recommended, just on this account, by those who there most favor it—as a great step towards the independence of this country. Now, I am not desirous that our acceptance of the scheme should go home to be cited (as it would be) to the people of England, as a proof that we so view it—a proof that we wish to be separated from the Empire. I am quite satisfied separation will never do. We are simply sure to be overwhelmed the instant our neighbors and we differ, unless we have the whole power of the Mother Country to assist us.

MR. SCOBLE—We shall have it.

MR. DUNKIN—I think we shall, if we maintain and strengthen our relations with the parent state; but I do not think we shall, if we adopt a scheme like this, which must certainly weaken the tie between us and the Empire. Our language to England had better be the plain truth—that we are no beggars, and will shirk no duty; that we do not want to go, and of ourselves will not go; that our feelings and our interests alike hold us to her; that, even apart from feeling, we are not strong enough, and know our own weakness, and the strength of the power near us; and that the only means by which we can possibly

be kept from absorption by that power, is the maintaining now—and for all time that we can look forward to—of our connection with the Mother Land. (Hear, hear.) We are told, again, that there are considerations connected with the Lower Provinces which make it necessary for us to accept this measure, that it is a solemn treaty entered into with them. Well, a treaty, I suppose, implies authority on the part of those who framed it to enter into it.

HON. ATTY. GEN. CARTIER—We are asking for that authority now, but you oppose it.

HON. MR. McGEE—Her Majesty says in her Speech from the Throne at the opening of the Imperial Parliament, that she approves of the Conference that framed the treaty. Is not the royal sanction sufficient authority?

MR. DUNKIN—Her Majesty's approval of those gentlemen having met and consulted together, is not even Her Majesty's approval —much less is it provincial approval—of what they did at that meeting. At most, the resolutions are not a treaty, but the mere draft of an agreement come to between those gentlemen.

HON. ATTY. GEN. CARTIER—Oh, yes, it is a treaty, and we are now fighting to uphold it.

MR. DUNKIN—Well, it is a draft of a treaty if you like, but it is not a treaty. Plenipotentiaries, who frame treaties, have full authority to act on behalf of their respective countries.

HON. ATTY. GEN. CARTIER—It is the same as any other treaty entered into under the British system. The Government is responsible for it to Parliament, and if this does not meet your approval, you can dispossess us by a vote of want of confidence.

MR. DUNKIN—The honorable gentleman may have trouble yet before he is through with it.

HON. ATTY. GEN. CARTIER—Very well, we will be prepared for it.

HON. J. S. MACDONALD—It is not so long since the honorable gentleman was voted out, and it may not be long before he is served the same way again. (Hear, hear, and laughter.)

MR. DUNKIN—Well, I was saying that this is no treaty to which the people either of Canada or of the Lower Provinces are at all bound; and it is very doubtful whether the people of the Lower Provinces will not reject it. I am quite satisfied that the people of Canada ought not to accept it, and I am not·

so very sure but that before the play is played out to the end, they will refuse to accept it, especially the people of Lower Canada, where, if it is carried at all, it will be by a very small majority. (Hear, hear.) But the honorable gentleman (Hon. Mr. CARTIER) has come over to my ground that it is not a treaty, but only the draft of a treaty, subject to the disapproval of the House and country. Taking it, however, as a treaty merely between those who entered into it, I am disposed to make one admission, that it has one quality such as often attaches to treaties entered into by duly constituted plenipotentiaries, and that is, that there seem to be some secret articles connected with it. (Hear, hear.)

HON. ATTY. GEN. CARTIER—The gentlemen who entered into it represented their governments, and the governments of all the provinces were represented. It is therefore a treaty between these provinces, which will hold good unless the Government is ousted by a vote of the House.

MR. DUNKIN—The honorable gentleman does not, I suppose, forget that when this Government was formed there was a distinct declaration made, that until the plan they might propose should have been completed in detail and laid before Parliament, Parliament was not to be held committed to it in any way. (Hear, hear.) But I was going on to something else, and I cannot allow myself to be carried back. I was saying that, assimilating this to a treaty like some other treaties, it seems to have secret articles in it. I find that one of the gentlemen who took part in the negotiations, the Hon. Mr. HATHAWAY, of New Brunswick—

HON. MR. McGEE — Mr. HATHAWAY was not here at all.

MR. DUNKIN—I was under the impression he was; though I acknowledge I have not burdened my memory with an exact list of the thirty-three distinguished gentlemen who took part in the Conference. At all events, he was a member of the Government of New Brunswick, which was a party represented at the Conference. Mr. HATHAWAY, at a public meeting lately, said that—

He occupied a very unenviable positio . He was under peculiar embarrassments, more so than any other speaker who would address them. It was well known to most of his audience that he had been one of the sworn advisers of His Excellency for the past three years. As such he could reveal no secrets of Council. It was true

H's Excellency had given him permission to make public the correspondence that had taken place on the subject of his resignation, but whatever might be the effect upon himself, there were secrets connected with the scheme that he could not divulge.

There were secrets of the scheme that he was not free to speak of. And we, too, find here that there are secrets; many matters as to which we may ask as much as we like, and can get no information. But the main point I was coming to is this. Call this thing what you like—treaty or whatever you please—it is not dealt with in the Lower Provinces at all in the way in which it is proposed to deal with it here. The Lower Provinces, we think, are smaller political communities than ourselves. Their legislative councils, their Houses of Assembly, we do not call quite so considerable as our own. We are in the habit of thinking that among the legislative bodies in the British Empire, we stand number two; certainly a great way behind the House of Commons, but having no other body between us and them in point of importance. (Hear, hear.) The Lower Provinces, I say, are not so big as we are, and yet how differently has our Parliament been treated from the way in which their smaller parliaments have been. And the apology, the reason assigned why we are treated as we are, is, that this thing is a binding treaty, if not yet between the provinces, at least between the governments of the other provinces and the Government of Canada. But how does the Lieutenant-Governor of Nova Scotia address his houses of parliament? " It is not my province," says he, " and I have no mission to do more than afford you the amplest and freest scope for the consideration of a proposal " —he does not call it a treaty—he calls it merely " a proposal, which seriously involves your own prospects." I suppose it does; but, so far from calling it a treaty, he does not call it even an agreement.

HON. ATTY. GEN. CARTIER—But what he says implies that he so regards it.

MR. DUNKIN—Does it? Let me read the whole passage :—

It is not my province, and I have no mission to do more than afford you the amplest and freest scope for consideration of a proposal which seriously involve your own prospects, and in reference to which you should be competent to interpret the wishes and determine the true interests of the country. I feel assured, however, that whatever be the result of your deliberations, you will deprecate attempts to treat in a narrow spirit, or otherwise than with dispassionate care and prudence, a question so broad that it in reality covers the ground of all parties, and precludes it from becoming the measure of merely one government or one party.

He gives his parliament perfect *carte blanche* to deal with it as they please.

Mr. WOOD—As a whole.

Mr. DUNKIN—It is a pity the same language was not addressed to us. In that case, Mr. SPEAKER, I think the motion put into your hands would have been, that you should now leave the chair, in order that we might go into committee of the whole to give the matter careful and becoming consideration. It is not pressed on in Nova Scotia, as it is here, with undue haste. The Lieutenant-Governor, in the next paragraph of his speech, goes on to say :—

I need only observe further, without in the least intending thereby to influence your ultimate determination, that it is obviously convenient, if not essential, for the legislatures of all the provinces concerned to observe uniformity in the mode of ascertaining their respective decisions on a question common to all. I have, therefore, desired to be laid before you some correspondence between the Governor General and myself on that point.

That correspondence, too, which is to be laid before the Parliament of Nova Scotia, has not been laid before us. (Hear, hear.) I have given the language addressed by this Lieutenant-Governor to his Legislature with reference to this "proposal." In what language do the Commons of Nova Scotia reply? How will they deal with it?

The report from the delegates appointed to confer upon the union of the Maritime Provinces, and the resolutions of the Conference held at Quebec, proposing a union of the different provinces of British North America, together with the correspondence upon that subject, will obtain at our hands the deliberate and attentive consideration demanded by a question of such magnitude and importance, and fraught with consequences so momentous to us and our posterity.

This, sir, is all that the Government of Nova Scotia ask the Legislature of that province to say. And I do not think that this course of theirs exactly indicates that they think they have made a treaty by which they must stand or fall, and to every letter and line of which they must force their Legislature to adhere. If they do regard it in that light, they have a very indirect way of expressing their ideas. But this is not the case merely in Nova Sco-

tia. In Prince Edward Island, every one knows the Government is not bringing this down as a treaty; in New Brunswick everybody knows that the Government has been more or less changed since the Conference, that a general election is going on, and that a great deal will depend on the doubtful result of that election. Every one knows that the matter is in a very different position in every one of the Lower Provinces from what it is in here; that there is none of this talk about a treaty anywhere but here. I would like, however, by the way, to draw the attention of the House for a moment to a case in which there undoubtedly was a treaty. I speak of the proceedings which eventuated in the union between England and Scotland. In the reign of Queen ANNE, at the instance of the two legislatures, then respectively independent—of England on the one hand, and of Scotland on the other—Her Majesty appointed commissioners to represent each of her two states, and they framed what were declared to be articles of a treaty. They took months to frame those articles; and twice in the course of their proceedings Her Majesty came down to assist personally at their deliberations. Their meeting was authorized by acts of Parliament; they were named by Her Majesty; they deliberated for months; and the Queen attended their deliberations twice. And after they had entered into this treaty—so called on the face of it—the Parliament of Scotland departed from it and insisted on changes which were approved of by the Parliament of England, and the treaty as thus changed went into operation. In both parliaments the bills to give effect to it passed through every stage; originated in Committee of the Whole, and had their first, second and third readings. All was done with the utmost formality; and yet there was there unmistakably a treaty solemnly made beforehand. Here we have an affair got up in seventeen days by thirty-three gentlemen who met without the sanction of the Crown, and only got that sanction afterwards. The document they agreed upon is full of oversights, as the Colonial Secretary states, and as everyone knows who has read it. Yet our Government regard it as a sacred treaty—though no one but themselves so regards it—and want to give it a sacredness which was not claimed even for that treaty between England and Scotland. (Hear, hear.) I am at last very near the close of the remarks I have to offer to the House; but I must say a few words as to the domestic consideration urged to force us into this scheme. We are asked, " What are you going to do ? You must do something. Are you going back to our old state of dead-lock?" At the risk of falling into an unparliamentary expression, I cannot help saying that I am reminded of a paragraph I read the other day in a Lower Province paper, in which the editor was dealing with this same cry, which seems to be raised in Nova Scotia as well as here—the cry that something must be done, that things cannot go on as they are. I have not his words here, but their general effect was this—" Whenever," says he, " I hear this cry raised, that something must be done, I suspect there is a plan on foot to get something very bad done. Things are in a bad way—desperate, may be. But the remedy proposed is sure to be desperate. I am put in mind of a story of two boys who couldn't swim, but by ill luck had upset their canoe in deep water, and by good luck had got on the bottom of it. Says the big boy to the little one, ' Tom, can you pray?' Tom confessed he could not call to mind a prayer suited to the occasion. ' No, Bill,' says he, ' I don't know how.' Bill's answer was earnest, but not parliamentary. It contained a past participle passive which I won't repeat. It was, ' Well, something must be done—and that—soon !' " (Laughter.) Now, seriously, what do honorable gentlemen mean when they raise here this cry that " something must be done ?" Is it seriously meant that our past is so bad that positively, on pain of political annihilation, of utter and hopeless ruin, of the last, worst consequences, we must this instant adopt just precisely this scheme ? If that is so, if really and truly those political institutions which we were in the habit of saying we enjoyed, which, at all events, we have been living under and, for that matter, are living under now, if they have worked so ill as all that comes to, or rather if we have worked them so ill, I think we hold out poor encouragement to those whom we call upon to take part with us in trying this new experiment. We Canadians have had a legislative union and worked it close upon five and twenty years, and under it have got, it is said, into such a position of embarrassment among ourselves, are working our political institutions so very badly, are in such a frightful fix, that, never mind what the prospects of this particular step may be, it must positively be taken ; we cannot help it, we cannot stay as we are, nor yet go back, nor yet go forward, in any course but just this one. (Hear, hear.) If

this thing is really this last desperate remedy for a disease past praying for, then indeed I am desperately afraid, sir, that it will not succeed. The hot haste with which gentlemen are pressing it is of ill omen to the deceived Mother Country, to our deceived sister provinces, and to our most miserably deceived selves. But the truth is that we are in no such sad case ; there is no fear of our having to go back to this bugbear past; we could not do it if we would. Things done cannot be undone. In a certain sense, whatever is past is irrevocable, and it is well it should be. True we are told by some of the honorable gentlemen on the Treasury benches that their present harmony is not peace, but only a sort of armed truce, that old party lines are not effaced, nor going to be. Well, sir, if so, suppose that this scheme should be ever so well dropped, and then that some day soon after these gentlemen should set themselves to the job of finding out who is cuckoo and who hedge-sparrow in the government nest that now shelters them all in such warm quiet, suppose there should thus soon be every effort made to revive old cries and feuds—what then ? Would it be the old game over again, or a variation of it amounting to a new one ? For a time at least, sir, a breathing time that happily cannot be got over, those old cries and old feuds will not be found to be revivable as of old. Even representation by population will be no such spell to conjure with—will fall on ears far less excitable. It has been adopted by any number of those who might otherwise be the likeliest to run it down. It will be found there might be a worse thing in the minds of many. Give it a new name and couple it with sufficient safeguard against legislation of the local stamp being put through against the vote of the local majority — the principle tacitly held so, and found to answer in the case of Scotland —and parliamentary reform may be found no such bug-bear to speak of after all. And as for the bug-bears of the personal kind, why, sir, after seeing all we have seen of the extent to which gentlemen can set aside or overcome them when occasion may require, it is too much to think they will for some little time go for so very much. Like it or not, honorable gentlemen, for a time, will have to be to some extent busy with a game that shall be not quite the old one. The friends of this project, Mr. SPEAKER, never seem to tire of prophesying to us smooth things, if only it is once first adopted. To every criticism on its many and manifest defects, the ready answer is, that we do not enough count upon men's good sense, good feeling, forbearance, and all that sort of thing. But, sir, if the adoption of this scheme is so to improve our position, is to make everything so smooth, to make all our public men so wise, so prudent, and so conscientious, I should like to know why a something of the same kind may not by possibility be hoped for, even though this project should be set aside. If we are to be capable of the far harder task of working out these projected unworkable political institutions, why is it that we must be incapable of the easier task of going on without them? I know well that in all time the temper of those who do not think has been to put faith rather in the great thing one cannot do, than in the smaller thing one can. "If the prophet had bid thee do some great thing, wouldest thou not have done it?" And here too, sir, as so often before, if the truth must be told, the one thing truly needed is what one may call the smaller thing—not perhaps easy, but one must hope not impossible—the exercise by our public men and by our people of that amount of discretion, good temper and forbearance which sees something larger and higher in public life than mere party struggles and crises without end ; of that political sagacity or capacity, call it which you will, with which they will surely find the institutions they have to be quite good enough for them to use and quietly make better, without which they will as surely find any that may anyhow be given them, to be quite bad enough for them to fight over and make worse. Mr. SPEAKER, I feel that I have taken up a great deal of the time of the House, and that I have presented but imperfectly the views I am anxious to impress upon it as to this great question. But for sheer want of strength, I might have felt it necessary, at whatever risk of wearying the House, to go into some matters more thoroughly, and more especially into that branch of the subject which relates to what I may call the alternative policy I myself prefer to this measure, and would wish to see adopted and carried out. As it is, I have but to say in conclusion, while warmly thanking the House for the attention and patience with which it has for so many hours listened to me, that I have said nothing but what I firmly believe, and felt myself bound to say, and that I trust the sober good sense of the people of these provinces, after full reflection and discussion, will decide rightly upon this the largest question by far that has ever been before them for decision. (Cheers.)